300

W, Horne

THE CENTURY PSYCHOLOGY SERIES

Richard M. Elliott, Gardner Lindzey & Kenneth MacCorquodale
Editors

Ingratiation

A Social Psychological Analysis

THE CENTURY PSYCHOLOGY SERIES AWARD
For 1963

Each year Appleton-Century-Crofts gives an award for a distinguished manuscript in psychology selected by the Editors of the Century Psychology Series. Considered will be works of two hundred typed pages or longer, which provide a significant contribution to the field of psychology.

EDITORS:
Richard M. Elliott
Gardner Lindzey
Kenneth MacCorquodale

1962 BERNARD RIMLAND
Infantile Autism: The Syndrome and Its Implications for a Neural Theory of Behavior

Ingratiation
A Social Psychological Analysis

EDWARD E. JONES
DUKE UNIVERSITY

New York

APPLETON - CENTURY - CROFTS
DIVISION OF MEREDITH PUBLISHING COMPANY

Preface

It has always struck me as curious and amusing that the student of homosexuality, drug addiction, or schizophrenia, is rarely asked why he became interested in the phenomenon that channels his scholarly energies, while I—a student of ingratiation —have been asked this question with great frequency. I have no wish to deny that the strategic side of social interaction is a source of endless fascination to me, but I will spare the reader any strained attempts to relate my intellectual curiosity about the topic to the themes of my human relations problems. It is better, and certainly of more general interest, to stick to a few of the objective landmarks in the development of the research to be described.

About five years ago, Keith Davis and I conducted an experiment in which subjects were induced to communicate a negative evaluation to a person who they thought was in the next room. We assumed, correctly as it turned out, that this task would create cognitive dissonance in the subjects—transmitting a hostile evaluation would be dissonant with the realization that the target person had done nothing to deserve it. We were able to show that if subjects were permissively coaxed rather than arbitrarily directed to read the derogatory message, their private impressions of the target person became more negative as a way of justifying their behavior. Shortly after completing the experiment we began to think of interesting next steps. A natural sequel to the experiment on the effects of delivering a negative evaluation would be a comparable experiment in which a positive evaluation would be involved. Subjects would be induced to give an evaluation which was more positive than they actually felt, and this might influence their private feelings about the target person.

We did not hasten to carry out this follow-up experiment because we did not think it would work. We were both intuitively convinced that inducing a subject to evaluate the target person more positively than he merited would arouse little if any dissonance. There are many ways for a subject to justify making such a benevolent appraisal. We commonly bias our public remarks in the positive direction from our private evaluations. The very commonness of this tendency to protect others from our negative attitudes began to intrigue me. It seemed to me that we knew very little about the circumstances behind this tendency to gloss over another's shortcomings in his presence, and that this was a neglected area in the study of social behavior. I had previously decided that I wanted to study the variables affecting self-presentation. As a student of social perception I had developed the not-very-startling conviction that our judgments of others are affected dramatically by the face they present to us. To understand social perception, therefore, it was essential to understand self-presentation. What better place to start than with presentations motivated by one's desire to create an attractive impression—to be ingratiating?

As a complement to my budding interest in the conditions which arouse ingratiation, it seemed to me that the issues involved in praise and winning favor were at least as intriguing if viewed from the perspective of the target person. How does one distinguish between genuine admiration and false praise? This was certainly a compelling instance of the difficulties of attributing intention or assigning causation on the basis of the content of communication alone. For the five previous years I had been championing the importance to the perceiver of the total interaction context in his attempts to evaluate the significance of particular acts, so I felt rather at home in extending this concern to the perceiver's problem of interpreting praise and making sense out of benevolent overtures.

As I now look back on the optimistic beginnings of the program to be reported in this monograph, I cannot escape the feel-

ing that my students and I unwittingly grasped a reluctant dragon
by the tail. Indeed, we were often thrown without ceremony in
our early attempts to induce subjects to flatter the target person
in a laboratory experiment. The plain fact of the matter is that
they balked at our initial efforts to induce a crassly manipulative
set and were indignant when, in post-experimental interviews,
we asked them if they were at any time tempted to take our
bait. We had touched an ethical nerve and were forced to use
experimental strategies which moved either in the direction of
explicit role-playing or in the direction of greater subtlety and,
alas, deception.

Our naiveté was somewhat overcome by corrective feedback
from these early research experiences, but the experiments which
followed were hardly immune from surprise endings or digressive
twists. My own conception of the antecedents and consequences
of ingratiation—as we began to call the tactical components of
social behavior—was considerably changed by the incoming experimental data. For example, I was unprepared for the potent
role played by self-deception in the service of our subjects' vanity.
The report that follows is anything but the unfolding of a carefully laid master plan of theoretical demonstration. I have written
it as much to try to understand the significance of our research
myself, as to share debatable insights and tentative conclusions
with others.

Much of the present monograph is built on the borrowed in-
sights and intuitions of friends, acquaintances, and colleagues.
Because ingratiation is ubiquitous and touches us all, I have tried
to widen my own perspective by considering the reactions to the
topic of many others in and out of the academic community. I
have benefited from the criticisms and suggestions of Kurt Back,
James Bieri, Peter Blau, Jack Brehm, Jerome Bruner, Arthur
Cohen, Morton Deutsch, Frances Dunham, Erving Goffman,
Albert Hastorf, Fritz Heider, Grace Heider, George Homans,
Edward S. Jones, Sidney Jourard, Alan Kerckhoff, Dennis Regan,
Leonard Reissman, and John Thibaut. The counsel of Harold
Gerard and Gardner Lindzey during the final stages of formula-
tion and writing was exceptionally helpful. As a token of my

gratitude to all of the aforementioned, I absolve them from any responsibility for the weaknesses in the final product.

I am especially grateful for the insights and arduous labor of several former students who—perhaps out of pity or just good humor—helped to sustain my conviction that ingratiation is a worthy topic of study. Kenneth Gergen and Keith Davis not only served as experimental assistants during the early phases of the research, but have continued to be sources of lively, constructive, criticism in reviewing various drafts of the present monograph. My debt to them and to Hilda Dickoff Perlitsh and Robert G. Jones is by no means covered by the many references to their names on the pages to come.

The bulk of the research reported herein was supported by a grant from the National Science Foundation. The enterprise would have been impossible without this financial support. The monograph would surely have been more slowly and painfully produced if I had not had the privilege of being a Fellow of the Center for Advanced Study in the Behavioral Sciences during the year 1963–1964. This Fellowship was primarily supported through a special grant from the National Institute of Mental Health. I am deeply indebted both to the Center and to the Institute for their support.

I wish, finally, to thank the American Psychological Association for permission to reproduce material from articles appearing in the *Journal of Abnormal and Social Psychology* and *Psychological Monographs,* and to thank the Duke University Press for permission to reproduce material from articles appearing in the *Journal of Personality.*

E.E.J.

Contents

THE CENTURY PSYCHOLOGY SERIES

Richard M. Elliott, Gardner Lindzey & Kenneth MacCorquodale
Editors

Ingratiation
A *Social Psychological Analysis*

1 Definition and Justification

The goal of the present monograph is to lay bare some of the more tactical or pragmatic features of social interaction. The focus is on the topic of ingratiation: its forms and guises, its antecedents, and its implications for social relations. The intent is neither to praise nor to censure ingratiation, but rather to give it a careful inspection and to locate its facets in the conceptual framework of contemporary social psychology. Toward this end, the present monograph considers the definition and taxonomy of ingratiation, includes a theoretical analysis of the conditions which favor or inhibit its practice, and features an account of several experiments designed to carry the inspection beyond anecdote and intuition.

Ingratiation, like its sister term, flattery, is mildly pejorative in everday usage. The word evokes connotations of dissimulation and deceit in social communication and self-presentation. We think of an ingratiating person as one who is over-concerned with the effects of his behavior on others, and under-concerned with the consonance between his behavior and the cognitions and feelings which support it. But the ambiguity of the term is highlighted when we read a drama review in which the critic assures us that so-and-so's performance was ingratiating. We take this to mean that he was winning and persuasive in his role, not that he was personally despicable or opprobrious. Can we assign a meaning to the term which will cut through the evaluative

1

atmosphere which surrounds it? This entire monograph is, in a sense, an effort to arrive at such a meaning, but the inquiry will begin with a direct confrontation of the definitional problem.

Our task is only incidentally that of providing a definition that fits established consensus or reflects current usage. We need a denotation that is consistent with a descriptive account of "ingratiating behaviors," and yet also anchors the term in psychological processes amenable to research. As the preceding paragraph suggests, there are bound to be problems associated with wrenching a term from its everyday context and assigning it status as a psychological concept. The matter is further complicated by the fact that the behavior with which we are concerned is interpersonal—it involves episodes defined by the intersecting cognitive and motivational systems of at least two actors. This means that we will be working with a class of social responses that may mean one thing to the actor, another to the target of the action, and still another to a neutral observer.

The best we can do is to try to restrict ourselves to one perspective at a time. We can then move on to define *ingratiation* as comprising those episodes of social behavior that are designed to increase the attractiveness of the actor to the target. The words "designed to" are critical in this definition, for it is the essence of ingratiation that it is directed toward increasing or maintaining attraction, whether this design is perceived by the actor, the target, or a neutral bystander. *Flattery* is a term which will be used more loosely when the securing of attraction is less important than the securing of benefit, and when over-generous praise is especially involved.

It may be contended immediately that this definition of ingratiation is hopelessly broad and inclusive, and that the desire for social acceptance and approval is always one of the motives affecting social action. In other words, as long as we choose to study the communications of well-socialized American adults, a focus on attraction-seeking behavior would seem the equivalent of a focus on all behavior emitted by one person in the presence of another. Any reasonable extension of reinforcement theory into the analysis of social interaction would surely emphasize the shaping of present actions by past reinforcements and, by implication, the shaping of action decisions by expected re-inforcements. Most theories of social structure make the strong assumption that persons accommodate their actions to social norms and that these norms are the shared expectations of the group. Such theories implicitly or explicity deal with the power of group members to impose sanctions and to constrain behavior in normative channels. Attraction-seeking, then, whether viewed as orientation to reinforcement or responsiveness to sanctions, seems to refer to ingratiation and much more besides.

What is needed in this attempt to frame a working definition of ingratiation is some notion of the normative base line from which ingratiation departs. The pejorative connotations of the term doubtless stem from the common consensus that ingratiation involves manipulative intent and deceitful execution. In short, ingratiation is a form of impression management or self-presentation which departs from normative expectations. It is the illegitimate and seamy side of interpersonal communication.

The base line of legitimacy, in the present case, is an implicit contract between the two (or three, or n) actors involved. There are many ways to describe this contract, and perhaps it is ap-propriate to start with the imprecise, but intuitively cogent, dramaturgical approach of Erving Goffman. Goffman (1955) feels that social interactions are permeated by expressive "ritual ele-ments." Not only is there communication in the traditional and narrow sense, but the communicators are also engaged in a "performance" as each gives cues about his definition of the situation, his view of himself, and his evaluation of the other. It is these expressive performance cues which establish in each actor an impression of the other's traits and motives. Perhaps the cornerstone of Goffman's position is his insistence that inter-actions are governed by the implicit agreement that each will help the other maintain face. Each actor enters into communica-tion hoping and expecting to act out a "line" with the tacit sup-port of the other. Whatever the purpose of the interaction, the participants claim for themselves a certain social value, a "face," which they work to maintain throughout the interchange. This involves the actor in "face-work"—actions which smooth over potentially embarrassing threats to the projected face and which make for coherence in the performance. The person thus has two points of view as he approaches and engages in the interaction—"a defensive orientation toward saving his own face and a protective orientation toward saving the other's face" (Goffman, 1955, p. 216).

Goffman tends to be more intrigued by the mechanisms actors use to maintain ritual equilibrium than by instances of ritual collapse. His discussion perhaps overemphasizes the silent conspiracy whereby each agrees to let the other play his chosen part. Nevertheless, the idea that there is a kind of implicit face-saving contract which governs social interaction is heuristic. At least it is instructive to treat ingratiation as a figure with such a contract as the normative ground. Ingratiation seems to involve a contract violation of a very special sort. It is clearly not the kind of violation represented by insults, cutting candor, or direct challenges to the other's face. Nor is it merely a matter of the quantity of deceit involved in face-maintaining gestures. We shall later see that the ingratiator may ply his arts by telling nothing but the truth (if not the whole truth) and that there may be much deceit involved in living up to the letter of the face-work contract. It is not the fact that a person lies or dissembles that marks him as ingratiating, but the fact that he exploits the face-work contract while seeming to validate it. The contract states that each will honor the other's claim to face, but this is presumably to be accomplished by developing a common definition of the situation which will support both faces. Ingratiation may be viewed as a subversive masquerade of this contractual bargain.

The exchange is subversive, rather than normative or ritual, because although the ingratiator's own perspective differs from the target person's, he gives signals indicating that he shares the latter's definition of the situation. He performs in the present setting to influence the definition of other settings in which he expects to be involved, while leading the target person to believe that the current setting is his primary focus. With considerable perceptiveness, Goffman suggests that "much of the activity during an encounter can be understood as an effort on everyone's part to get through the occasion and all the unanticipated and unintentional events that can cast participants in an undesirable light, without disrupting the relationships of the participants. And if relationships are in the process of change, the object will be to bring the encounter to a satisfactory close without altering the expected course of development" (1955, p. 229). The ingratiator has a broader temporal perspective. He supports the target person's definition of the situation by his own communicative behavior, but he adds a few twists which accelerate the target person's own face-work. This is because he privately places the present situation in the context of other, future encounters with the target person. Because he is intent upon building a beneficial relationship, he desires to leave the present interchange with a better face than when he entered it. As a result, subsequent encounters can start from a new, and for him more gratifying, level of social interchange.

What seems to be involved in this extension of Goffman's description of face-work is the emergence of non-normative behavior under a normative guise. The notion of a face-work contract carries with it the implication of reciprocation or exchange. When one person supports another's line, he establishes a claim that his own line be supported. The relationship between ingratiation and the more legitimate processes of face-protection may be further clarified by examining two explicit treatments of social interaction as an exchange.

One such treatment is that of George Homans (1961), who presents a frankly economic or profit-centered view of interpersonal relations. Human beings, like pigeons in a Skinner box, are so constructed that they will act to maximize reward and minimize cost. When this well-worn assumption is placed in the context of social interaction we are informed that "the open secret of human exchange is to give the other man behavior that is more valuable to him than it is costly to you and to get from him behavior that is more valuable to you than it is costly to him" (p. 62). The next step in Homans' argument is the recognition that one person may come to expect more profit from an exchange than the other, and both may agree that this is just. This would be the case if the first person had more *investments* than the second, that is, more education, expertise, age, beauty, or other forms of social capital. Following closely the analogy to economic exchange, Homans proposes a general rule of *distributive justice:* "A man in an exchange relation with another will expect that the rewards of each man be proportional to his costs—the greater the rewards, the greater the costs—and that the net rewards, or profits, of each man be proportional to his investments —the greater the investments, the greater the profits" (p. 75).

While the ramifications of this proposition will not concern us here, the rule of distributive justice may be viewed as another version of the normative contract which serves as the backdrop for social interaction. When distributive justice does not obtain, the person who is disadvantaged will display anger and the person who is advantaged may feel guilty (cf. Adams, 1963). The contract to which Homans' rule alludes is more fundamental and abstract than the contract implied by Goffman's discussion of face-work, but they function in a similar way to throw the distinctive features of ingratiation into relief. While the face-work contract was used in the foregoing discussion to emphasize the dual frame of reference of the ingratiator, the distributive justice contract brings more explicitly into focus the facet of moral or normative obligation. While the ingratiator depends for his effectiveness on the responsiveness of the target person to the norm of distributive justice, he himself sets out to violate this norm. In various ways he attempts to stretch his profit margin in the interchange so that it exceeds what might be expected given the costs he incurs and the investments he brings to the situation. Taking our lead from the component concepts stated in the distributive justice rule, the ingratiator may pursue any of the following strategies, singly or in combination:

1. He may attempt to reduce or minimize the *costs* he incurs in eliciting rewards from the target person, while informing the target person that these costs are high. This practice may be easily seen in many industrial settings where workers try to deceive their supervisors concerning the level of difficulty or the amount of time and energy their work requires. By analogy, the more perfunctory and indiscriminate flattery is, the more obvious it will be that this is low-cost behavior, and the less effective it will be.

2. He may attempt to falsify his *investments* by, for example,

presenting his background and his abilities in a favorable light. Since the person with higher investments "deserves" the greater profit, this becomes a usable strategic maneuver in stretching one's profit margin. It is, of course, important that the investments claimed by the ingratiator are so perceived by the target person, and herein lie many of the subtle problems of impression management to be discussed in subsequent chapters.

3. He may attempt to increase the *reward* value that his behavior has for the target person. It is crucial, for example, that compliments and praise should be judiciously administered rather than squandered. The ingratiator must not satiate the target person since he has a clear interest in maintaining the latter's hunger for compliments and agreement. Some of the implications of this interest will be dealt with in later discussions.

In these three ways the ingratiator may obligate a target person who is committed to the distributive justice rule. In order to live up to the implications of the rule, the target person must find ways to benefit the ingratiator, to act in his presence in a more gratifying or reinforcing way.

One difficulty in relating the concept of obligation to the concept of ingratiation is that a tension of obligation may or may not be an effect of increased attraction. Person A may obligate person B by gifts or favors, and B may feel compelled to reciprocate even though he is not in the least attracted to A. This kind of exploitative bargaining is closely related to, but not synonymous with ingratiation. The ingratiator seeks to affect the bargaining process not merely by falsifying his contributions to it, but by managing to create an attractive impression which in turn influences the terms of the exchange. Obligation and attraction are, however, clearly related since friendship incurs obligations of both a general and a specific nature. It might be said that the ingratiator is ultimately concerned with creating feelings of obligation which will redound to his benefit, and he chooses the management of attraction to achieve this goal because an obligation based on friendship is more stable and secure than an obligation built on temporary advantages in the exchange process. In fact, the readiness to accept an apparent loss in the exchange may, itself, win a friend. The ingratiator may win approbation as a person for his apparent willingness to continue in the exchange at an "unjust" disadvantage to himself. In so doing he exploits the distributive justice rule.

A better insight into the role of the influence-through-attraction factor in the broader context of interpersonal exchange can be gained from a fresh look at the model of interaction proposed by Thibaut and Kelley (1959). While their treatment has many features in common with that of Homans' (1961), for our purpose it has the advantage of more sharply delineating the structural basis of interpersonal exchange.

Thibaut and Kelley maintain that a relationship developing between two persons will take the form dictated by the pattern of outcomes or rewards available to each and to varying degrees under the other's control. Each person has a repertory of responses he is capable of making, and interaction occurs when a person emits certain responses in *his* repertory in close proximity to certain responses emitted by another. In a metaphoric sense, portions of the two repertories intersect and there will be variations in outcome as a function of the particular responses which come together in time. Thibaut and Kelley elaborate on this metaphor by viewing the two repertories as the rows and columns of a matrix. Person A's responses may be arrayed at the head of n columns and person B's responses may be arrayed to the left of m rows. There are thus a total of n times m cells in the matrix, and each cell represents a potential co-occurrence of a response in A's repertory with one in B's repertory. Out of the response combinations that actually occur, certain outcomes are generated for each actor. At each point of response intersection—that is, in each cell of the matrix—we may picture two entries representing the outcome values for each person when the two responses in question occur in close proximity. We may be flexible about whether these are actual outcomes which have been experienced in past interactions between A and B, whether they are expected outcome values, or whether they are some combination of expected and known outcomes. A, of course, is in a much better position to know or to predict his own outcomes in a particular cell than to predict B's outcomes. But insofar as his own outcomes are contingent on B's responses, self-interest will force him to take account of B's outcomes in some way. Like Homans, Thibaut and Kelley assume that each individual will try to maximize the goodness of his outcomes during the interaction—or rather, optimize the outcomes since maximal outcomes are rarely attainable and interaction inevitably involves compromise. He will, therefore, adjust his behavior to increase the likelihood of his landing in those cells in which his own outcomes are optimal. If both persons have high outcomes in the same cells (indicating a high correspondence of outcomes), then the interaction will naturally gravitate toward those cells. If there is low correspondence of outcomes, the relationship may either break up or take the form of a give-and-take, take-and-give exchange.

By means of such a matrix model, which of course severely simplifies the underlying reward structure of even the briefest interaction episode, it is easy to depict variations in power within the relationship. In the Thibaut and Kelley formulation, if one person has more to gain and more to lose in the relationship than the other, he has greater dependence on the other and the other therefore has greater power over him. The person who has greater power in this sense can get the other person to do things for him—he can call forth certain responses out of the other's repertory because of his superior capacity to reward and punish. There can of course be different patterns of power and counter-power (each may have certain kinds of power over the other) and the potential for power may be distributed in different ways within the matrix, but our essential concern at this point is only with the broad outlines of the model.

If we now imagine that A has the potential power to move B through a wide range of outcomes, B will naturally try to behave in ways approved by A in order to secure the more positive outcomes in the range. A is thus in a position to reinforce compliance, to dictate the cell in which their joint responses will land them. The Thibaut and Kelley analysis is primarily devoted to the implications of different matrix entries—different power combinations—for predicting compliance, norm formation, and other social phenomena. Their analysis takes the values in the matrix as a hypothetical given and then considers the implications of different distributions of these values.

The preceding account of the workings of a dyadic matrix suggests that a person who is relatively low in power can increase the goodness of his own outcomes through behavioral compliance with the high-power person's wishes. Our interest in ingratiation, however, alerts us to the possibility that there are other ways in which the relatively powerless person can obtain better outcomes in the long run. Compliance, as the term has been used above, merely verifies the understanding of both persons concerning the outcome pattern existing in the matrix, and represents essentially an exchange of goods or services. Ingratiation, however, is directed toward the redistribution of outcome values in the matrix. Rather than representing a fair exchange within the limits of the matrix, it involves an attempt to introduce extraneous considerations into the application or utilization of available power.

A further distinction not made explicit by Thibaut and Kelley is the distinction between the total response repertory of person A (or B) and that portion of each repertory which is considered relevant during a particular interaction episode. While each person is potentially free to make any response of which he is physically capable, the setting (as defined by the participants) brings forth a certain range of response possibilities and suppresses others. The ingratiator, in effect, tries to expand the boundaries of relevance. He introduces responses from the irrelevant portions of his total repertory to complicate and influence the character of the pertinent sub-matrix. He attempts, essentially, to bias the responses of the target person in the ingratiator's favor and to neutralize those responses delivering negative outcomes by the strategy of introducing extraneous considerations.

The ingratiator's immediate objective is to modify the criteria affecting the target person's action decisions—especially those having strong consequences for the ingratiator's satisfaction. But this is only the first step in a two-step process. The ingratiator's ultimate objective is to equalize power in the relationship. The first step temporarily blunts the application of power, but the second step involves a change in the value of outcomes with which the ingratiator can provide the target person. His goal in expanding the relevant repertory is to manage a favorable impression with materials and on grounds other than those supposed to be involved in the exchange. To take one simple example, he may try to amuse his boss with a joke during a conference, thus taking time which might have been spent in fulfilling the stated conference purpose of detailing market conditions in the Dubuque area. Insofar as such "extra-curricular activities" succeed, he becomes attractive in the target person's eyes; and an important consequence of this gain in attractiveness is an enhanced ability to control the target person.

Implications for a working definition. The preceding discussion may now be briefly summarized by extracting and emphasizing some of the common features of the foregoing approaches to social interaction. The term ingratiation—it may now be stated more explicitly—refers to *a class of strategic behaviors illicitly designed to influence a particular other person concerning the attractiveness of one's personal qualities.* Ingratiating actions are illicit because they are directed toward objectives not contained in the implicit contract which underlies social interaction. We have adapted the models of Goffman, Homans, and Thibaut and Kelley to help in specifying the nature of the illegitimacy involved. Each of these models brings to light a slightly different facet of the concept in question. With the help of Goffman's description of the face-work process it was possible to dramatize the degree of overlap between actions required by certain norms of courtesy and actions in the service of ingratiation. It was suggested that subtle variations in normative signals are exploited by the ingratiator for their value in producing ulterior social effects. With the help of Homans' concept of distributive justice, the exchange concept was explicitly introduced and with it the concept of obligation and its relation to attraction. Finally, by extending Thibaut and Kelley's picture of intersecting response repertories to include a distinction between relevant and irrelevant responses, we have been able to highlight the ingratiator's use of irrelevant responses to effect an ultimate change in the value of relevant ones. Combining these contributions, we may conclude that ingratiation is an illegitimate member of the social exchange family because the ingratiator presents himself as a party to one kind of exchange—with one set of terms and conditions—while in fact he is primarily involved in another kind.

EXPERIMENTAL METHOD
AND OPERATIONAL DEFINITION

Nothing has yet been said about the specific responses which fall into the ingratiation class. The working definition just proposed focuses on the strategic intent of ingratiating acts and not their observable characteristics or identifying criteria. Indeed, a special paradox exists in the attempt to bring ingratiation under empirical control. Since ingratiation is built on a deceptive exploitation of the target person's understanding, the scientific observer may also be deceived. The ingratiator will naturally attempt to keep his "illicit design" concealed. By what special talents or devices can the scientist bring this design to light?

The answer, reflected in the studies to be reported, is that the scientist is in a better position than the target person to gain insight because he uses precise and replicated comparisons. Through the facilities of experimentation it is possible to pose different subjects with different self-presentational problems, and to observe and record their solution attempts. Most of the studies presented in this monograph follow this approach by experimentally varying the subject's condition of *dependence* on another subject. Primarily through the use of differential instructions, subjects in one treatment are placed in the position of needing another person's approval or attraction. They need this attraction for reasons which vary from experiment to experiment. In one case, the subjects are led to believe that the experiment being conducted is a prelude to a lucrative and exciting one to follow, but entry into the second experiment requires pairs of subjects who are definitely attracted to each other. In another case, the subjects are told that eventually they will work as a team and are led to believe that the attractiveness of each to a certain other person will be made public knowledge. In every case the subject has something to gain *if* the other person in the experiment finds him attractive.

For reasons of comparison, subjects in a contrasting experimental treatment are placed in a position of minimal dependence on another person. They are, for example, told that the other person's ability to judge personality is under scrutiny and that they are to serve as stimulus persons in a study of first impressions. By instructional emphasis it is made clear that their task is to be true to themselves, to convey a valid picture of their attributes so that the "perceiver" has a chance to do well.

By dividing the experiment into treatment groups within such different contexts of interaction and by attempting to hold all other factors constant, it is possible to identify the phenomena implied by the working definition of ingratiation. All subjects are given the same opportunity for controlled communication with another, but subjects in a given treatment group face the problem either of creating a positive impression or of conveying valid information about the self. In treatment conditions emphasizing the former problem, the subject is presumably motivated to elicit attraction in a short time span, with limited communication tools. Having implanted by instruction an intent to create an attractive impression, we may observe the subject's responses in the service of this intent. There remains the question of whether such an operational approach captures the feature of illicit design contained in the working definition. This question is difficult to answer given the particularities of the experimental setting. In a sense the "high-dependence" instructions give the subject license to plot, manipulate, and deceive—at least they lead him to the waters of deceit, though they do not force him to drink. It may seem strange to question the legitimacy of the subject's behavior when we have provided the incentive to make him especially conscious of his social effect. On the other hand, the subject has a stake in concealing his motives from the target person. Furthermore, he has a certain amount of freedom in interpreting the actual situation of communication and in signaling his interpretation to the other person. Thus, even in the ingratiation or high-dependence condition, the communication occurs in a setting of "getting-acquainted." The subject's problem of presenting a favorable impression cannot be completely detached from the constraints implicit in the normal getting-acquainted process. With this consideration in mind, we may say that illegitimacy is involved to the extent that the subject modifies his normal getting-acquainted responses to effect the purpose of making himself more attractive. The extent to which he does this may be crudely estimated by a comparison of high- and low-dependence conditions.

The experimental approach, as briefly described above, would seem to have all the disadvantages of an inductive, bootstrap operation. Since we do not know exactly what to include under the heading of ingratiating behavior, and since we do not wish to prejudge the situation, we propose to create the conditions under which ingratiation *should* occur and then call the resulting responses ingratiating. But we are not primarily engaged in a search for indices of ingratiation so that we may better identify them in the casual encounters of real life. Our strategy is a comparative one, and it seems clear that behavior which would have an ingratiating basis in one setting could have a different motivational basis in another setting. Our main interest is in exploring the relation between certain antecedent conditions and certain consequent responses within the area of strategic, effect-oriented social behavior. This exploration involves a certain amount of naive induction, as reflected in the difficulty of always being able to specify the particular dependent variable most likely to show the effects of independent variations. But there are obviously theoretical considerations involved in the choice of experimental operations and in the making of predictions concerning their likely effects. Our general strategy, then, is to use experimental methodology as an aid in the comparison and elimination of alternative explanations, but to retain flexibility in the description and analysis of the resulting response data. This strategy seems to recommend itself during the early stages of investigating such an evanescent and complex topic as ingratiation.

A strategy of concealed or participant observation of social behavior in natural settings seems precluded until the terrain is better mapped, and the antecedents and the behavior topography of ingratiation are better known. But could not the interview or the detailed phenomenological exploration of remembered incidents of flattery and conformity be used as a method of inquiry? It is our judgment, based on several informal attempts to do this, that the interview is not particularly fruitful even when used as an adjunctive method of inquiry. Ingratiation and related topics are designed to arouse defensiveness in any interviewee. Even if one could penetrate the public (external) aspects of this defensiveness by adroit questioning, one would still have to cope with the problems of self-deception and self-justification. In fact, such "autistic distortion" seems so prevalent that a subsequent chapter shall be devoted to relevant evidence on the issue.

WHY INGRATIATION?

There are many tempting courses to follow in justifying the decision to study ingratiation. We might begin with the assertion that, since ingratiation is an ubiquitous social phenomenon, we study it for the same reason Mallory tried to climb Mt. Everest—because it is there. Both the omnipresence and the importance of ingratiation are quite dramatically confirmed by observing what happens when the topics of flattery, manipulation, and deceptive social tactics are introduced into casual conversation. A common reaction to the intrusion of such topics is an almost palpable discomfort or at least ambivalence. There is often considerable interest in pursuing the theme, and it readily captures conversational attention; at the same time, however, there is an undercurrent of uneasiness which becomes more and more pronounced as the conversation continues. There seems to be something ultimately disruptive about making the arts and stratagems of impression management salient and putting them on public display—even when everyone is obviously trying to be "detached and objective."

A more valid reason for studying ingratiation is that light might be shed on other common social phenomena such as the antecedents of group cohesiveness, the conditions of social influence and conformity, and the significance of social reinforcement in sequences of social interaction. To glance at each of these areas in turn, many of the experiments on group cohesiveness, a few years ago, attempted to produce momentary feelings of mutual attraction in a group by experimentally manipulating perceived similarity, common goal orientation, or the complementary needs of the members. Few questions were raised in the cohesiveness literature concerning the reasons why these manipulations strengthened group cohesiveness—if, indeed, they did. From the large amount of literature on social influence and conformity, we know much about the conditions which affect submission and resistance to the expressed judgments of others, but we know next to nothing about the tactical "bribes" which may be involved in soliciting agreement, their costs and their consequences. Studies of verbal operant conditioning have demonstrated the ease with which reinforcements provided by the experimenter can "shape up" the behavior of a subject, but the investigators involved in this research have been slow to ponder the implications of the fact that this is an interpersonal event involving all the intricacies of mutual social control.

An even more general and compelling reason why ingratiation merits investigation is because the topic brings into relief some of the central mysteries of social interaction. The more we learn about ingratiation, the better will be our understanding of the intricate interplay between social perception and social action. In focusing on the ingratiator's tactical problems—his self-presentational dilemmas—we at the same time illuminate the obverse problems of one who wishes to present himself with sincerity and to convey valid information to another concerning his feelings and opinions. In studying the target person's problem of discriminating between ingenuous and manipulative acts, we can perhaps gain insight into the more general problem of perceiving motives or attributing intentions. In addition, the analysis of power and status differences seems incomplete without some attention to the tactical buffers and ploys available as instruments of power as well as instruments of the erosion and deflection of power.

The social interaction between two human beings is a strange and wonderful achievement. Linked to others only by all the subtleties of interpersonal communication, each of us must somehow adapt to an environment the basic characteristics of which are ultimately inscrutable. And yet, effective social behavior rests on the individual's ability to perceive the dispositions (attitudes, beliefs, motives) of others, to sort out information about such dispositions from information about position and role, and finally to predict behavior by understanding how dispositions and role requirements interact. The more discerning and veridical these perceptual and cognitive achievements, the more the individual benefits in his adaptive preparations for effective action.

People need each other and are oriented toward each other for a great variety of reasons. Some of these reasons are especially pertinent in any discussion of the implications of ingratiation. A decade ago, Festinger's theory of social comparison processes stressed the important role that other persons continually play in defining the "world out there" and in helping a given individual measure his abilities (Festinger, 1954). Festinger argues that we constantly use others, both explicitly and implicitly, as informants about the environment and our capacities for action in it. The role of others as informants is especially important in those realms of action where nonsocial means for testing reality are not available. If an individual wishes to know whether a diamond is harder than glass, he may perform the operational test of scratching one upon the other. If he wishes to know how fast he can run, he may stake out some known distance and record his time in traversing it. But there are broad areas of belief validation and ability assessment within which such direct tests are not possible or feasible. In particular, there are many personal qualities—friendliness, respectability, moral courage—which can *only* be assessed by social means or mirrored in the reactions of others to us. It is with respect to these areas of irreducible human uncertainty that social comparison or the use of information about and from others is especially important. In view of the fact that the vast majority of personal attributes about which one might seek information have an evaluative significance, one begins to see why valid social comparison may be threatened by recurrent intrusions of ingratiation.

One of the weaknesses of the theory of social comparison processes is that Festinger is forced to point to two separate drives in the area of ability evaluation. First of all, the individual has a drive to know exactly where he stands and what he is capable of achieving. Secondly, the individual (in our culture at least) has a drive to increase his abilities, to improve from one occasion to the next. To picture these two drives as jointly exerting pressure on the individual is to say that he may often find himself caught between the need for valid information and the need for pleasant information. If he really strives to measure himself as a "total person" in an unbiased way, he runs the serious risk of finding that he is wanting. If he deliberately selects those sources of information likely to give him support, he of course loses any assurance that the information is valid.

It is this dilemma of self-presentation which grows out of the individual's potentially incompatible desires to learn objectively about himself and to be judged favorably. The wish to be judged favorably causes him to present himself in ways which are likely to have a special appeal for those doing the judging. But the very specialness of the appeal reduces the informational value of a gratifying judgment received. Ideally, the individual may discover that he is loved and/or respected in different social contexts, though his presentations are always based on a firm self-concept and never consciously designed for their social effect. At the other extreme, the individual may fail to construct a valid self-identity because approval from others is always associated with deliberate and artful attempts to win it. It is assumed that most of us fall in between these two extremes but close enough to the second so that the dilemma of self-presentation has the ring of familiarity.

On the other side of the coin there is an even more formidable obstacle to informed and valid self-knowledge. In the realm of those underlying qualities which comprise an individual's own essential worth as a person, the information available to the individual is apt to be clouded because of the *informant's* motives in the situation. Thus, if the person genuinely wishes to determine what others think of him—and we have argued that he is likely to experience conflict in this wish—he would have a difficult time finding out. The same motives that push him toward the management of an attractive impression in the eyes of others, push the others toward seeking attraction in his eyes. Since one of the first rules of being attractive is to be supportive and agreeable, the person is not likely to see himself, and his worth, clearly reflected in the communications presented to him by others.

The preceding discussion suggests, then, that a strong inclination towards hypocrisy pervades and biases interpersonal relations. Ingratiation and the related activities of face-work generate a considerable amount of mischievous noise which masks and distorts feelings and judgments as they are conveyed across the interpersonal chasm. Lest this appear to be too searing an indictment of a part of our common fate, however, let us briefly examine the more constructive role played by ingratiation in the realm of group functioning and group locomotion.

If we concentrate on the distinctive illegitimacy of ingratiation in contrast to face-work and other normative hypocrisies, it is not easy to uncover a constructive function for the class of actions being considered. In the long run, at least, it is probably never constructive for one person to take advantage of another's definition of their common situation. However, if we broaden our discussion to include those behaviors which are often ingratiating in intent—for example, compliments and opinion conformity—a few important positive features emerge.

In order for a group to take concerted action, the members must first move toward unequivocal agreement about the task situation and the actions required to cope with task requirements. Insofar as decision-making power is unevenly distributed within the group, and insofar as responsibility or accountability is correlated with decision-making power, the leader(s) will and should play a larger role in defining the situation than the followers. Whether or not the leader has the capacity to make appropriate decisions on behalf of the group, he is the one who suffers most if an inappropriate decision is reached. Since his own actions are so important in performing a task successfully, anything which affects his capacity to act with confidence and decisiveness will have clear implications for such success.

Compliance in the execution of task directives is, of course, essential for task completion or group locomotion, but ingratiating overtures from follower to leader presumably go beyond "you're-the-boss" compliance. Such overtures symbolize the follower's recognition of the existing power structure and contribute to a spirit of harmony and group cohesiveness. As we shall see in chapter three, a person tends to bring his private feelings in line with his public actions. As a consequence, ingratiating compliments may be transformed into attitudes of respect. In this manner, ingratiation can lead indirectly to a condition in which the leader has the solid support of his followers and, most important of all, is aware of that support. Such support enables the leader to formulate and steer action in an atmosphere of trust and security. It expands the area of his free movement while at the same time making his followers and their welfare salient.

Perhaps it seems peculiar to propose that trust can be an outcome of hypocrisy, especially considering the traditional view of the leader's problems in developing such trust. Thibaut and Riecken (1955), for example, argue that as a person's power position in a group improves, he tends to lose information concerning the *spontaneous* loyalty and good will of his subordinates. The powerful person cannot know whether the compliance of his subordinates is merely a reflection of his own power and his own surveillance over them, or whether his subordinates would have complied without being kept under surveillance. Without questioning the plausibility of this argument, it is possible to suggest that ingratiating behaviors help to create the illusion of spontaneous good will and that this illusion often becomes a reality. Even if the leader has doubts about the genuineness and representativeness of the ingratiating follower's behavior, he does learn something about the latter's allegiance to the power structure and he may see the ingratiating behavior as a signal that the follower will continue to be submissive and will not threaten his leadership status. Whether or not the illusion becomes a reality, the leader is sustained by being the target of ingratiation and, because this sustenance makes him more secure, he may be capable of performing with greater decisiveness and creativity.

A final comment is in order concerning the role of compliments in producing group cohesiveness. Compliments may symbolize a kind of identification with the group as an entity and may lend support to the existing distribution of power, although they do not necessarily bring people closer together. Farson (1963) argues that praise often functions to establish a distance between two people rather than to draw them together. Praise not only carries an implication of status difference, in that the praiser seems to be claiming some capacity to judge or evaluate the other, but praise in the form of compliments may generate tension and embarrassment in a social situation. To the extent that praise does help to keep people apart, the role of ingratiation in group functioning takes on another aspect. Compliments and praise among followers, between followers and leader, and between leader and followers, may actually function to neutralize and mask those feelings which might otherwise erupt and interfere with group performance. It is conceivable that praise and compliments serve to maintain an optimal interpersonal distance so that a group can maintain itself as a group, while avoiding the substitution of consummatory interpersonal relations (hostility, love) in actions relevant to a task. This suggestion is quite compatible with Freud's view that group relations become viable through the inhibition and sublimation of direct libidinal expressions (Freud, 1921).

PLAN OF THE PRESENT MONOGRAPH

The preceding discussion was an attempt to present, in an informal and unsystematic way, some of the difficulties involved in defining ingratiation, the implications of these difficulties for operational analysis and measurement, and finally some reasons why the topic seems to merit investigation. Having thus set the stage, we shall proceed to a more detailed analysis of the phenomena of ingratiation. Wherever possible, we shall try to buttress our position with data from controlled experiments. When this is not possible, however, we shall not hesitate to speculate—hopefully disciplining our speculations by convincing phenomenological analysis and illustrating them by appropriate anecdote. The reader is hereby invited to disagree when the analysis is not persuasive and is challenged to design a study to decide between the competing speculations.

In chapter two, we shall take a taxonomic look at the behaviors which often serve ingratiation. Our goal in chapter two is purely descriptive; it is designed to bring into consideration the range of behavioral phenomena which must be kept in mind when selecting measures of dependent variables in the planning of an experiment.

Chapter three addresses itself to certain aspects of the individual's self-presentational dilemma: one who manipulates the affections of another increases his power over the other but loses information about the appeal of his unvarnished self. The role of autistic distortion is introduced as a common tendency which narrows the horns of the dilemma or, perhaps more accurately, blurs the dilemma's focus.

Chapter four attempts to lay bare the cognitive and motivational substructure of ingratiation. The analysis is quite formal and it casts the ingratiation episode in a model emphasizing the incentives involved in an exchange of outcomes, the subjective probability of successfully increasing one's outcomes through attraction-seeking strategies, and the perceived legitimacy of attempting to curry favor. These three sets of factors are presumed to interact as conditions affecting the onset and course of ingratiation.

In chapter five we confront directly the fact that dependence, or the relative absence of interpersonal power, is a major condition for the occurrence of the kinds of tactical behavior we call ingratiation. It seems obvious that the low-power person should be more highly motivated to use such tactics than the high-power person, but this chapter goes beyond the obvious to show (a) that ingratiation may occur "downward" in a status hierarchy and will, when this happens, take a different form from "upward" ingratiation, and (b) whether or not upward ingratiation will occur depends on the dependent person's estimates of the possibility of gaining more favorable outcomes.

In chapter six we take an intensive look at the coin's obverse as we shift from considering the conditions which arouse and channel ingratiating behavior to considering the conditions which affect the reactions of the target person. As we would expect, the same principles which govern the decision to be ingratiating have a bearing on the effectiveness of the ingratiation attempt after launching. However, there are interesting points of disjunction in applying the same principles because of differences in perspective on the part of the ingratiator and his target person. Chapter six dramatizes the problems of mutual perceptual adjustment and shows that there are apt to be systematic errors in the ingratiator's predictions of his probable effectiveness *and* in his interpretation of the target person's actual response.

In chapter seven, we shall attempt to assess what the analysis has accomplished and to raise questions for future research in the area of interpersonal behavior strategy.

2 *Tactical Variations in Ingratiation*

Ingratiation can, according to the present definition at least, take all or any of the forms by which interpersonal attraction may be solicited. When one considers the great number and variety of target persons toward whom ingratiating overtures might be directed, and the many interaction contexts in which such overtures might occur, it is clear that any attempt to develop a check list of specific "effective" tactics would be fruitless. It is probably true in general, however, that when we are dealing with ingratiation we are largely concerned with communicative behaviors which reflect the communicator's view of himself, aspects of the surrounding environment, and his esteem of the target person. In considering the kinds of communication which might achieve this purpose, we suggest that there are three major classes of ingratiation tactics: other-enhancement, opinion conformity, and self-presentation. We shall consider each of these in turn, along with a possible fourth class, that of giving gifts or rendering favors.

COMPLIMENTARY OTHER-ENHANCEMENT

The first class of tactical variations involves communication of directly enhancing, evaluative statements. This class of tactics probably comes closest to the meaning of flattery in its everyday usage. The ingratiator finds ways to express a high, positive, evaluation of the target person and emphasizes the latter's various strengths and virtues. He may distort and exaggerate the target person's admirable qualities to convey the impression that he thinks highly of him, but such direct duplicity is by no means an essential ingredient in behaviors of this class. The ingratiator may call attention to positive attributes which do, in fact, characterize the target person, but through errors of omission he may fail to develop the negative side of the ledger. Again, while it is fruitless to specify the particular responses which are likely to bring attraction out of other-enhancement, we may single out this class of tactics as one designed to convey the impression that the ingratiator thinks highly of the target person.

The effectiveness of other-enhancement as a tactic in the service of attraction-seeking seems to derive from the premise that people find it hard not to like those who think highly of them. Such a premise is accepted as a Gestalt axiom of social life by Heider, who declares that a dyad is unbalanced if one party likes the other, but is disliked by him (1958, p. 202). Heider's system is designed to reflect the phenomenal world of the reference person; therefore, if one person perceives that the other likes or respects him, that one person will have a tendency to move toward liking the other. If no such movement occurs, the target person will feel the subjective discomfort or strain that imbalance can bring. In data taken from many different groups in many different settings, Tagiuri (in Tagiuri and Petrullo, 1958) found a recurrent strong relationship between liking someone and perceiving that the someone reciprocated the attraction—or in his terms, between choosing and guessing the choices of others. This high degree of congruency between sociometric choice and guess, while not particularly surprising, provides empirical support for the Heider balance axiom. While it is no more plausible to conclude that the perception of being liked causes liking than to conclude that liking someone results in perceiving that the other reciprocates the attraction, congruence is presumably a result of both kinds of developments. A study by Jones, Gergen and Davis (1962) shows that subjects change in the direction of greater attraction toward a stimulus person who expresses his approval of them as persons. The fact that other experimental studies with similar results could be cited leaves little room for doubt concerning the effect that perceiving attraction has on becoming attracted in return. The tactic of other-enhancement seems well rooted in the psychology of interpersonal attraction.

Our present focus on the use of compliments as an ingratiation tactic directs us to inquire into the *means* whereby one person convinces another that he admires or likes him. Curiously enough, the tactical problems are logically the same whether the one likes the other or not—it is the perception of being liked, not the actual fact of being liked, which is the crucial factor linking other-enhancement and attraction-seeking. Regardless of his private feelings about the target person, the ingratiator must present his "enhancing" compliments in a manner which assures or promotes their credibility. In most cultural contexts there are firm moral constraints against attempts at other-enhancement which stem from manipulative intentions. The sycophant cannot afford to have his true motives discovered, and (as we shall soon see) usually manages to conceal his ulterior intentions from himself. As an aid to concealment both from himself and from the target person, the effective enhancer wishes to establish the appropriate motivational context for his complimentary communication. This might be done by playing down his dependence on the target person in order to reduce the suspicion that he needs or expects to be benefited by him. This may be a matter of timing his remarks so that they occur in a context where the benefit desired is not a salient issue at that moment. Establishing the appropriate motivational context may also involve waiting for, and contributing to, states of "approval deprivation" so that compliments rendered will be more gratefully received.

One way to create a context for credibility is to arrange to have the compliment mediated by a third party. The advantages of such a strategy were early noted by Lord Chesterfield who recommended to his son the ". . . innocent piece of art; that of flattering people behind their backs, in the presence of who, to make their own court, much more than for your sake, will not fail to repeat and even amplify the praise to the party concerned. This is, of all flattery, the most pleasing and consequently the most effectual" (Dunne edition, 1901, I, p. 179). We suggest that it is the "most pleasing" because credibility is established through the mediation process—there is in such cases no clear evidence that the originator of the compliment wanted or expected to have the compliment repeated.

It also seems obvious that, regardless of the context of the other-enhancing communication, credibility is affected by the inherent plausibility of the compliment. Outlandish or clearly unwarranted compliments are likely to prove embarrassing to the recipient and unlikely to secure the desired attraction. But it is not sufficient for the tactician to be merely credible. The communicator must deliver compliments which are more lavish than the recipient expects or thinks he deserves, and yet he must convey the impression that he himself believes them to be justified. Alternatively, he may settle for creating the impression that his compliments were well meant and selflessly motivated even though he may be perceived as stretching the point a little. If the communicator attributes characteristics about which the target person is himself quite certain and secure, the communicator may establish his credibility without necessarily increasing the esteem in which he is held. Or, if the communicator convinces the recipient of his praise that he, the recipient, really is a noble and virtuous fellow, there would be certain paradoxical effects. The more highly the recipient thinks of himself, the less he needs support from others, and the more justified and matter of course their compliments become. Lord Chesterfield puts the matter in a most engaging way:

Men have various objects in which they may excell, or at least would be thought to excell; and, though they love to hear justice done to them, where they know that they excell, yet they are most and best flattered upon those points where they wish to excell, and yet are doubtful whether they do or not. . . . The late Sir Robert Walpole, who was certainly an able man, was little open to flattery upon that head; for he was in no doubt himself about it; but his prevailing weakness was, to be thought to have a polite and happy turn to gallantry; of which he had undoubtedly less than any man living; it was his favorite and frequent subject of conversation; which proved, to those who had any penetration, that it was his prevailing weakness. And they applied to it with success (Dunne edition, 1901, I, p. 27).

At this point, there exists a pair of quite contradictory propositions: a person will like an admiring other to the extent that the person admired has high self-esteem *or* to the extent that he is dissatisfied with himself and hungers for reassurance. If one considers carefully the implications of Heider's balance theory, he would be forced to restrict his claim that perceived liking begets liking to those cases in which the person likes or places a high value on himself. In the theoretical development of their study, Deutsch and Solomon (1959) took the next logical step by predicting that when a person is led to have a low opinion of himself, he will tend to like another person who shares that low opinion. As Deutsch and Solomon point out, this tendency toward balance operates jointly with a "positivity effect"—that is, an additional tendency to like those who approve of you and to dislike those who disapprove, regardless of your level of self-evaluation. In their experiment, which involved the manipulation of a subject's success or failure followed by the receipt of an approving or disapproving note from another "team member," they found circumstantial evidence for the joint operation of these effects. Thus a subject was most positive toward one who wrote an approving note, and most negative toward one who wrote a disapproving note, after the subject had succeeded. Receiving an approving or a disapproving note after failure resulted in impressions of intermediate favorability. While both the balance theory derivation and the Deutsch and Solomon extension seem plausible, a quite contradictory alternative would suggest that people are especially pleased when other-enhancing compliments are directed toward their weaknesses. It is, so the argument might run, especially here that support from others is needed and will be maximally appreciated. Such an argument seems to underlie Lord Chesterfield's recommendation that the flatterer concentrate on the target person's weaknesses rather than his strengths. Nor is there a lack of empirical support for this alternative, though most of it is quite indirect and concerns reactions to criticism rather than approval. Jones, Hester, Farina, and Davis (1959), for example, found that subjects with low self-esteem were much more inclined than subjects with high self-esteem to rate negatively a student who had derogated them. Rosenbaum and deCharms (1960) found that low self-esteem subjects were more negative in appraising someone who had verbally attacked them than were high self-esteem subjects.

Unfortunately, it is possible that in some circumstances the two contradictory "self-esteem hypotheses" may cancel each other out, with the result that one's self-evaluation appears to be irrelevant. Dickoff (1961) found that one's impressions of another are favorably affected by the amount of approval received, but that one's initial level of self-esteem does not affect the correlation between amount of approval received and impression granted. Thus her results provide support neither for the balance hypothesis nor for the hypothesis that low self-esteem persons show more gratitude for favorable feedback about themselves. The existence of the "positivity effect," on the other hand, was strongly confirmed in her study.

We are a long way from being able to specify the conditions under which these alternative hypotheses hold or to conclude that each is pervasive in its operation and somehow holds the other in check. For purposes of the present discussion, the issue might be tentatively resolved by stressing the role of uncertainty in the target person's response to compliments. This is clearly a part of Chesterfield's analysis, for it is a person's *doubts* about an attribute in which he wishes to excel which render him open to flattery. This statement suggests an interpretation of the Deutsch and Solomon results. If a person is quite convinced that he is poor in some ability, or unworthy in some area, compliments which tell him that he is good in that ability or area will appear incredible to him and raise suspicions of ulterior motivation. Certainly every effort was made in the Deutsch and Solomon study to convince the subjects that they had in fact succeeded or failed, and the notes conveying approval or disapproval must have varied in their credibility as a function of the experience they followed. For this reason, perhaps, we see little evidence that the failing subject is especially drawn to one who writes him an approving note. To the extent that a person is uncertain about an attribute he would like to possess, however, or to the extent that he needs reassurance about such an attribute, he presumably will respond to flattering compliments concerning the attribute with increased attraction for the communicator. The sophisticated and artful flatterer may become an effective lay practitioner of this uncertainty reduction principle, making sure, of course, that the uncertainty is always reduced in the positive or favorable direction.

Commitment and the criteria of evaluation.   In forecasting the most likely effects of his own behavior, the would-be ingratiator must realize that the acceptance of a complimentary evaluation is a function both of the criteria on which it seems to be based and of the extent to which the evaluation involves a commitment to present or future actions. Turning first to the criterion problem, it stands to reason that the more differentiated and discriminating the compliment, the more its validity may be precisely judged by the target person. The ingratiator may enhance his credibility by complicating his endorsement of the target person in various ways. One way of doing this is to concoct a judicious blend of the bitter and the sweet. Thus the ingratiator may acknowledge negative attributes in the target person of which the latter is fully aware and then go on to emphasize positive attributes of which the target person is uncertain. Such a tactic is clearly related to the use of the two-sided message in persuasive communications (Swanson, Newcomb, and Hartley, 1952, I and E division, pp. 506–519). Some risk is involved since the tactic requires that the ingratiator correctly intuit the target person's certainty about his own weaknesses and his willingness to acknowledge them.

Another way of complicating the endorsement in the interests of credibility is to avoid the use of ambiguous absolutes in favor of relative comparisons. The target person may be pleased to learn that the ingratiator judges him to be good on some dimension, but a compliment which specifically locates him as better than others he respects is apt to be more compelling and gratifying. What we are referring to here is the extent to which a compliment involves "weasel words" that can mean one thing to the communicator and another to the target person. As an aside it may be noted that many recommendation forms now require comparative or percentile judgments in addition to general remarks about a candidate's qualities. In the academic community, if not in other contexts as well, professors are so likely to ingratiate on behalf of their job-seeking protégés that such procedures are designed to force them to be more discriminating. (Whether these forms succeed or not is a moot question.) One of the obvious factors underlying the target person's preference for comparative judgments of worth is the fact that such judgments involve more of a commitment on the part of the communicator. Unless the ingratiator is totally unprincipled, target person A may justly assume that the ingratiator will not tell him he is better than B and then tell B he is better than A. A major position of the present monograph is that ingratiators do things which conceal their ulterior motivation from themselves. For this reason, flattery and ingratiation tend to operate in a hinterland of ambiguity—where quick retreat is possible and where truth is difficult to verify. Also for this reason, the ingratiator who risks the dangers of being unambiguous may be that much more effective.

The role of commitment may be more clearly seen when the gesture intended to enhance another involves action with important consequences for the actor. Perhaps no compliment is as meaningful as being chosen on the first go-around, being given a clear promotion to a prestigious position, or a raise which is out of line with expectations. But here we are obviously on the borderline between ingratiation and fair exchange, since there is something inherent in these examples which implies that the target person's services are at least as valuable to the complimenter as his affection or respect. In keeping with our definitional discussion of the last chapter, however, it is to the ingratiator's tactical advantage to exploit the exchange process or the underlying norms of distributive justice. It cannot be ruled out, then, that raises are sometimes given for the gratitude and affection they purchase or that team choices may have ulterior significance as part of a strategy of winning friends.

A paradoxical consideration in the giving of compliments is the information revealed concerning the complimenter's expectations. If a person is lavishly complimented on some performance, he may very well conclude (depending on the context) that the complimenter had a rather low general opinion of him and may still have it. An important part of the context, presumably, is the target person's own view of the discrepancy between the particular performance and his level of ability. But it seems to be true that the better a person becomes at something, the less likely he is to receive compliments from those who have formed firm prior opinions of his ability and have established high expectations for him. This may help to explain the rather precarious position that athletic champions occupy in the public eye. Spectacular performances become routine and the "off day" may generate thunderous boos. It may also help to explain the commonly observed depressions of college freshmen who find it hard to adjust to the process of being evaluated by a higher and more demanding standard.

Returning to the notion that compliments may be more effective when they are comparative rather than absolute, the ingratiator may set the stage for his compliments by establishing in the eyes of the target person his own high standards for evaluating performance. This may be done, as implied above, by running down others in comparison or by criticizing initial performance efforts and by praising later ones. If these two tactics are used together, the paradoxical effect described above is not likely to occur. The target person will accept the compliment as hard won for his having met high standards and will not view it as a condescending gesture merely confirming the complimenter's low general evaluation of the target person relative to others.

Mention should be made at this point of a recent (and as yet unpublished) experiment by Aronson and Linder. By an ingenious procedure, subjects were exposed to brief evaluations of themselves delivered by another person (a confederate of the experimenter) in a series punctuated by brief subject-other interactions. The subject was led to believe that the confederate was unaware that he, the subject, was in a position to monitor the incoming appraisals.

The confederate was best liked in a condition in which his early appraisals of the subject were uncomplimentary but became quite positive over time. The subject's evaluations were significantly more favorable in this "negative-positive" condition than they were in a "positive-positive" condition characterized by uniformly complimentary appraisals. Since the confederate presumably did not realize he was being overheard by the subject, the appraisals in the uniformly positive condition could not realistically be viewed as deliberately flattering by the subject. It may be that the subject preferred the negative-positive confederate because his praise represented more of a hard-earned victory, won from a competent and discerning person who does not give praise easily. Aronson and Linder also suggest that the initial negative appraisal is upsetting to the subject and that the ultimate positive appraisal produced greater final liking because it reduced a high-drive state. As suggested earlier, the ingratiator may make his compliments count far more by first arousing a condition of approval deprivation. Aronson and Linder present internal evidence to show that the more the subject acknowledged being upset in the negative-positive condition, the more favorable were his final evaluations of the confederate. These closely related interpretations—evidence of competence and drive-state reduction—will be considered further in subsequent discussions of the effectiveness of various ingratiation tactics.

Also relevant in this context of establishing credibility is the fact that other-enhancement may paradoxically be expressed by apparent deflation of the other, as evidenced by the phenomenon of the friendly insult. Masculine small talk, especially, is frequently peppered with barbs, derogation, and sarcasm. The recipient of a friendly insult is given notice that he (a) has the attention of the communicator and (b) has the strength and good nature to survive such an attack. He may also infer from the tone and the context that the insulting comment is actually inapplicable to him, for if it were true it would never have been offered. Friendly insults serve another purpose as well: they provide a contrasting backdrop for the expression of occasional (but nevertheless highly important) positive comments. Such comments from one who is known for his caustic wit and malicious sense of humor are all the more significant to the recipient.

Spontaneous versus fished-for compliments. Perhaps one of the poorest ways to find out what others think of us is to ask them. There are, of course, settings in which one person may seek and obtain a valid appraisal of himself from another. Physicians, employers, teachers, family members, and close friends may comment candidly on certain of our foibles as well as our virtues. By and large, however, when people ask us what we think of them—either generally or on some specific dimension—they do not necessarily crave the truth. We have already commented in the preceding chapter on the fact that people want both accurate and pleasant information about themselves and that they are therefore ambivalent about seeking out information sources that might convey unpleasant truths. When we are asked for our opinions about another, we often sense that they would prefer our compliments to our candor and act accordingly—for either humanitarian or devious reasons. Undoubtedly the target person himself is aware that the more avidly he seeks information from others the more invalid it is likely to be, since it is commonly understood that such information-seeking is often motivated by the need for support rather than by the need for genuine appraisal. In any event, it would seem that the ingratiator, bent on convincing a target person of his genuine admiration for him, would arrange to deliver spontaneous compliments as well as to respond with praise whenever the bait is offered. In fact, the ingratiator may learn from the fishing-for-compliments episodes just what the target person's areas of uncertainties are and exploit this knowledge in subsequent spontaneous praise.

CONFORMITY IN OPINION, JUDGMENT, AND BEHAVIOR

A second class of tactics available to the ingratiator is that which involves conforming in various ways to the target person. Experimental investigations into the conditions of conformity have been numerous during the past decade, and we now know a great deal more about the nature of conformity than we did at the end of the Second World War. The bulk of these studies, however, have focused on conformity as a response to social influence pressures rather than as a tactic of social influence in its own right. Those who have emphasized the fact that conformity tends to increase when opinions are monitored by one or more target persons, over the level of agreement when there is no such monitoring (e.g. Deutsch and Gerard, 1955), have recognized the factor of attraction-seeking or attraction maintenance. But the present discussion makes even more emphatic the possible role of conformity in securing attraction and deals with agreement and imitation as witting or unwitting strategies of ingratiation.

Whereas the tactic of other-enhancement attempts to capitalize on the proposition that persons like those who appear to like them, the conformity tactic follows another proposition: persons like those whose values and beliefs appear to be similar to their own. Like the earlier proposition, the present one is clearly stated by Heider (1958) as an interpersonal axiom and strongly supported by abundant research evidence showing that similarity of values and interests leads to selective association and mutual attraction (e.g. Newcomb, 1961). The tactic of opinion conformity ranges from simple agreement with expressed opinions, through more elaborate attempts to articulate the position presumed to be held by the other, to the most complex forms of behavior imitation and identification. Thus there may be much or little cost incurred by the conformity tactician since the tactic may involve complex diagnostic work or simple reflexive agreement. The more elaborate forms of conveying similarity of beliefs or opinions are often the most effective but also the most difficult and costly to initiate and maintain. Even the most casual concessions to the opinions of another may be emotionally or cognitively costly if the new opinions must be maintained over extensive time periods. Public agreement which coexists with private disagreement should in itself produce cognitive dissonance, especially when the new opinion must be maintained in front of those other than the primary target (if only because the latter is present and attending) and when it requires adjustments in related opinions. The fact that opinion conformity has these repercussions may provide some basis for the aphorism, "imitation is the sincerest flattery." It is judged to be sincere precisely because it tends to be psychologically costly.

The relationship between conformity and ingratiation is not a simple one. On the one hand, if a person likes the one who shares his beliefs and opinions and there is nothing more involved, then the goal of the conformist is to convey his genuine, independently derived agreement with this person. It is also quite possible, however, that ingratiation may be furthered by manifest opinion *change*. In some contexts, the ingratiator may be liked more by the target person if he starts out with a divergent opinion but is gradually converted to the target person's position, than if he starts out agreeing with the target person. This tactic is one way by which the conformist can advertise the psychological costs incurred. In giving up an opinion after showing a certain amount of resistance, the belated conformist may be perceived as paying a costly tribute to the target person's superior wisdom and he may, therefore, be rewarded with the attraction he seeks.

Gerard and Greenbaum (1962) present interesting evidence in this connection. We have already suggested that compliments are especially effective if the recipient is uncertain about the degree to which he possesses the attribute being complimented. Gerard and Greenbaum's data provide support for a similar conclusion in the area of judgmental uncertainty. In their experiment, each subject was confronted by repeated disagreement from two of three peers on a series of judgments concerning unambiguous stimuli. The judgments of these two peers always preceded the subject's judgment, while the third peer's judgment always followed the subject's. The third peer either agreed with the subject on each judgment, agreed with the first two and disagreed with the subject, or, depending on the treatment condition, he began to agree with the subject after initially disagreeing with him for varying periods of time. Once he began to agree with the subject he continued to agree with him from that point on. Lateness of the "switch" to agreement was the experimental variable. There were four subjects in each of 12 conditions ranging from "early switch" to "late switch."

Gerard and Greenbaum were primarily interested in the subject's impression of the peer whose judgment followed the subject's as a function of the point at which the latter began to agree with him. They found, of course, that the subject was most unfavorable in his evaluation of the peer when the latter always disagreed with him. It was also found that the subject was most favorable when the peer always agreed with him. Data from the "switch" treatments showed that the peer was liked relatively more when the switch was quite early or quite late than when the switch was moderately late. Gerard and Greenbaum argue that positive evaluation of the early switcher has the same basis as affection for the peer who always agreed: because we have learned the value of allies in past attempts to interpret reality, we generally like those who appear to support our views. Positive evaluation of the late-switching peer contrasted sharply with the negative evaluation of a peer who never switched. Gerard and Greenbaum suggest that the relatively positive reaction to the late-switching peer is a function of the degree of uncertainty reduction which he provides at this point. Presumably the longer the subject goes without an ally, the more uncertain he becomes. The subjects rated their judgmental confidence on each trial and there was clear evidence that confidence decreased the greater the number of trials on which the subject was confronted with unanimous disagreement. It was also true that the later the switch the greater the *increment* in confidence on the trial immediately following the switch.

If we were to view the subject as the target person and the third peer as the potential ingratiator, the Gerard and Greenbaum findings suggest that consistent conformity *or* conformity preceded by sufficient resistance to raise the target person's uncertainty, are both effective stratagems for gaining approval. In one case uncertainty arousal is prevented, in the other it is reduced after reaching an uncomfortable extreme. The uncertainty reduction hypothesis may be seen as a special case of the drive reduction hypothesized in the negative-positive condition of the Aronson and Linder study (see above).

As Gerard and Greenbaum point out, the increased attractiveness granted in the late-switch treatments may also have been due to an assumed contingency between the subject's behavior and the peer's switch. A derivation from dissonance theory (supported by Aronson, 1961) is that subjects become attracted to objects to the extent that effort was expended in acquiring them. This would help to account for the greater liking of the negative-positive versus the positive-positive confederate in the Aronson and Linder experiment. It also might account for the Gerard-Greenbaum results. The object in the Gerard and Greenbaum study was agreement from the third peer, and the subjective experience of effort may relate to the amount of resistance which the subject had to overcome—the lateness of the switch. While this alternative is a possibility, the fact remains that uncertainty is great during the later trials before the switch, markedly reduced by the late switch, and the positive impression of the late-switching peer is quite consistent with an uncertainty reduction hypothesis.

The ingratiator's success in managing to express opinions which are similar to the target person's would appear to be an effective tactic whether or not there is any perception that the similarity is the result of a change in opinions. Indeed, it seems intuitively obvious that the lower the status of the ingratiator relative to the target person, the more the effectiveness of the conformity tactic depends on concealing any evidence that a conforming *change* in opinions has occurred. This may be accomplished by occasional disagreements in unimportant areas, or by attempts to anticipate as yet unexpressed opinions of the other person. For example, if the ingratiator strongly criticizes the President of the United States before the target person has expressed his own negative feelings, the target person will probably not question the sincerity of the ingratiator. The target person would have occasion to be more suspicious of an adaptive or tactical change to the extent that he had previously made his own position clear. This suggests that an important resource for the sophisticated tactician is his ability to deduce unstated opinions from stated ones. This is especially important, presumably, when the tactician is lower in status than the target person.

The advantage of being able to express opinions similar to the target person's before the latter has made his known is confirmed in a study by Jones, Jones, and Gergen (1963). In that study subjects listened to a dialogue between two other students.

One student, Mike, always agreed very closely with the other, Paul, in expressing his opinions on a variety of issues. In half of the cases, Mike went first and Paul second; in the remaining cases the sequence was reversed. In predicting Paul's feelings about Mike, subjects predicted more positive evaluations when Mike expressed his opinions first. They saw Mike as much more conforming and manipulative when his opinions were given in response to those of Paul. The opinions actually expressed by Mike were identical in the two cases.

We might comment, finally, on the tactical value of differential conformity and the bases for deciding the crucial issues on which conformity is most likely to win the attraction that is sought. Again we may follow up an implication of Festinger's social comparison process and suggest that the target person is likely to be most appreciative of agreement when he wants to believe that something is true but is not sure that it is. Since slavish or indiscriminate agreement may be transparent and therefore fall of its own weight, the sophisticated tactician may be more successful in his ingratiation attempt by combining disagreements in trivial or unimportant areas with agreements on those issues in which the target person needs support for a shaky but congenial conviction. It is at this point that the earlier-stated principles governing selective other-enhancement coincide, in effect, with the principles of differential conformity.

A related basis for deciding when to conform and when not to conform is the relevance of the opinion issue to the relationship and to the business to be transacted therein. A study by Schachter (1951) showed that more pressure toward uniformity is generated on issues relevant to the group's goals than on issues that are less relevant. While there is little additional evidence that bears on this point, Festinger (1954) states as a corollary of his social comparison theory, "The greater the relevance of the opinion or ability to the group, the stronger will be the pressure toward uniformity concerning that opinion or ability" (p. 132). In chapter six, we shall present detailed evidence indicating that high-status ingratiators conform more on irrelevant issues while low-status ingratiators conform more on relevant ones. For the moment, we conclude with the suggestion that an effective ingratiation tactic would be to establish credibility by disagreeing mildly on irrelevant issues and to win attraction in safety by agreeing enthusiastically on relevant ones. The problem of defining relevance may, of course, be extremely difficult in some relationships, and the notion of relevance does not lend itself neatly to operational realization as an experimental variable.

SELF-PRESENTATION

A third tactic of ingratiation involves the explicit presentation or description of one's own attributes to increase the likelihood of being judged attractive. In the present context self-presentation refers both to those communications which are explicitly self-descriptive: "I am the kind of person who . . . ," "One of my weaknesses is . . . ," "Compared to most men I am . . ."; and to more indirect communicative shadings which convey the same kind of information about how a person wishes to be viewed by others.

In speculating on the uses to which self-presentation may be put in the service of ingratiation, it seems obvious that there are many kinds of impressions to be avoided in a particular culture. In the American adolescent culture, for example, a person reduces his attractiveness to others when he conveys an impression of boastfulness and conceit, of rudeness and lack of consideration, of spitefulness and malice, or of deceit and crass opportunism. Therefore, the successful tactician wants to avoid sending out cues which point to any of these attributes. Beyond this, however, there are many subtleties which determine the attractiveness of one's projected self. In attempting to gain another person's favor, the ingratiator must consider that person's idiosyncratic preferences and those commonly associated with persons in his role or position, as well as the values embraced by the general culture. That is, the ingratiator should present himself in different ways as a function of his perceptions of the target person's likes and dislikes, the more so, the more motivated he is to be accepted by the target person. In this context, then, the ingratiating person is one who models himself along the lines of the target person's suggested ideal, or at least who communicates his success in approximating this ideal.

This point has a general significance which underlies the entire range of tactics that may be employed by an ingratiator. The decision to communicate other-enhancing compliments, for example, will be affected by perceptions of the target person's vanity. Whether or not conformity will be effective as a tactic for winning favor depends on the target person's values concerning social accommodation and congeniality versus ruthless candor in interpersonal relations. In chapter six we shall see this last proposition supported in an experiment by Jones, Gergen, Gumpert and Thibaut (in press).

There are two distinct and quite contradictory forms that self-presentation may take in the interests of securing the favor of another. A person may present himself in such a way as to advertise his strengths and virtues, or he may present himself in such a way as to enhance by implication the strengths and virtues of the target person. In the preceding chapter we derived from Homans' (1961) distinctions the suggestion that a person may lay a claim to preferred outcomes in an exchange if he is able to convince the other of his high "investments." The term investment was not formally defined, but we followed Homans in pointing to such attributes as age, education, expertise, and other ingredients of what might be called social status. If the ingratiator can convince the target person that he brings valuable investments to the interchange, he will presumably be looked upon with greater respect and admiration than he might otherwise have been. This would place him in a better position to influence the target person on his behalf. Jones, Gergen, and Davis (1962) and Gergen (1962) found that female undergraduate subjects responded to instructions encouraging them to make themselves attractive to another person by describing themselves very favorably—significantly more favorably than when instructed to be their natural selves. We may tentatively conclude that exaggerating strengths and minimizing weaknesses is the prepotent response to instructions emphasizing the creation of a positive impression, though the empirical generality of this proposition is unknown and it is certain that a caveat of *ceteris paribus* should be attached.

There are certain risks involved in such self-enhancement or investment advertisement. The credibility of a self-description is obviously an all-important condition for its effectiveness in establishing a face or a claim to certain investments. Then too, a person who attempts to enhance himself in competition with, or at the expense of, another, is unlikely to elicit attraction or preferred treatment for his efforts. Self-enhancement often carries with it implications of invidious comparison with the target person. The obverse of self-aggrandizement is of course self-deprecation or humility, which has its own value as a tactic of ingratiation. By emphasizing his weaknesses and lack of investments, a person reduces the likelihood of being considered a competitive threat and he aligns himself with such important cultural values as modesty and objectivity of self-appraisal. Confessions of weakness increase one's dependence on a relationship and render one vulnerable to exploitation, but one's dependence may also make salient the norms of *noblesse oblige* and the Christian ideal of the strong helping the weak. Modesty, humility, and the acknowledgment of one's dependence may derive their effectiveness as ingratiation tactics from their contribution to an implicit other-enhancement. This is especially clear when one emphasizes one's inadequacies in the process of asking for advice or assistance. Such requests generally imply admiration or respect for the potential advisor. Because such appeals for advice play directly on the vanity of the recipient, Plutarch (Goodwin edition, 1889) felt that this was a particularly insidious form of flattery.

In much the same manner, one who reveals intimate personal experiences or feelings to another implies respect for the other's understanding, tolerance, or discretion. One also implies by such intimate self-revelation that one does not fear exploitation by the target person, that one trusts him, and that one would like the relationship to continue and deepen.

Since self-enhancement and self-deprecation are clearly contradictory presentational tactics, it is important to establish the conditions under which one is more effective than the other and vice versa. One important factor is the obviousness and the

security of the ingratiator's investments. If a person is widely
acknowledged to be the best in his field, if he wears a star on
his shoulder, if it is clear that he comes from a "first family,"—in
short, if his high investments are undeniable public knowledge—
he will be more ingratiating if he does *not* stress these investments, but instead responds with modesty and humility in front
of the target person. If, on the other hand, the investments of the
potential ingratiator are low, uncertain, or unknown to others, he
will be inclined to emphasize his positive attributes and conceal
his weaknesses. We are not suggesting that low-investment or
low-status people will describe themselves more positively than
will high-investment people. What we are saying is that those
whose investments are obvious will become modest when motivated to seek attraction, and those whose investments are uncertain will become more immodest under such motivation. As
we shall see in chapter six, an experiment by Jones, Gergen, and
Jones (1963) provides qualified support for this hypothesis.

It should not be assumed, of course, that persons attempting
to create a favorable impression always make some basic decision
either to exaggerate their strengths or to play them down. Common sense tells us that people are generally going to strike some
kind of balance in delineating positive and negative attributes
of the self. To say nothing but good things about oneself clearly
smacks of conceit and exaggeration; constantly to stress one's bad
features vexes and embarrasses the listener, generally leaving
him with no response beyond repetitive reassurance. The psychologist's task of developing predictions about self-presentation
is one which involves specifying the conditions which determine
the general favorability of one's self-depiction *and* the particular
pattern of attributes which are acknowledged and denied.

RENDERING FAVORS

A logical candidate for the status of an ingratiation
tactic is the giving of favors, since persons are likely to be attracted to those who do nice things for them. The main question
is whether the rendering of favors is fruitfully viewed as an

ingratiation tactic or whether it is simply a case of open social exchange—one person obligates the other by performing a service at some cost in a context where the norms of distributive justice presumably apply. Attraction might or might not be a byproduct in such a case. Ingratiation involves more than the manipulation of obligation; by our definition, attraction is illicitly sought, and any favors the ingratiator hopes to obtain are the consequence of having made oneself attractive. In certain cases, a favor or gift is presented under conditions which make reciprocation in kind difficult or impossible. The only available response of the recipient might be attraction for the other person because of his selfless generosity. An ingratiator might take advantage of such a possibility and make himself more attractive without benefiting in any other way from his generosity. While this possibility exists, the essential factor in such an award of attraction seems to be the self-reflecting value of the favor or gift under the given circumstances. It therefore seems that the ingratiating significance of the presentation of gifts and favors can be dealt with under the heading of self-presentation and that no separate category is required. It should not be concluded, however, that gifts and favors are unimportant in the cementing of friendships or in the more general context of social influence. To paraphrase Homans, we influence others to give us the things we want more than they do, by giving them the things they want more than we do. In chapter four, a more formal analysis of this exchange process will be undertaken in an attempt to clarify the relationship between legitimate social exchange and ingratiation.

SUMMARY

In the present chapter we have attempted to lay out an informal taxonomy of those tactics which may, and often do, operate in the service of ingratiation. Establishing such a taxonomy, if only in the most preliminary form, is a prerequisite for research planning and the search for dependent variables appropriate to given experimental conditions. While acknowledging that almost any observable act or gesture can serve, on occasion, to create a more or less favorable impression in the eyes of the observer, we proposed that other-enhancement, conformity, and self-presentation are the three most obvious classes within which tactical responses fall. With respect to responses in each of these classes, the primary problem of the ingratiator is to convince the target person that his communications are not unduly shaped by pragmatic considerations and are congruent with the ingratiator's private convictions. The content of the communication and/or the context in which it is presented must be so arranged as to establish the credibility of the communicator. To be effective in eliciting attraction, however, the communication must be more than merely credible. It must represent an idea, judgment, or position in which the target person wishes to believe, but about which he is to some extent uncertain. Other-enhancing compliments are, then, most effective when addressed to such desirable but uncertain attributes. Conformity is most likely to be gratifying to the target person if it represents support for a personally important but controversial opinion. Self-presentations may also be designed to make the target person feel secure in his own position or self-judgment. Especially under conditions where a person's status or power (his investments, in Homans' terms) are equivocal, however, the individual may respond to pressures to make himself attractive by immodest emphasis on his strengths and virtues. Gifts and favors may be exploited by the ingratiator to secure attraction, but this may be viewed as a kind of self-presenting behavior and the significance of favors for ingratiation seems amply covered by including them under the heading of self-presentation.

3 Self-Deception, Vanity, and the Significance of Approval

We have stated that the ingratiator seeks to be judged attractive. He so arranges his communicative behavior to create a positive impression in another person. His interpersonal actions are thus shaped by strategic considerations and directed toward the achievement of certain social effects. It is our purpose in the present chapter to show how easily the average person can be induced to behave in instrumental, effect-oriented ways, how readily he can deceive himself into believing he has not done so, and how his hunger for approval seems to be the infectious factor underlying this autistic self-deception.

GOALS MEDIATED BY ATTRACTION

As a way of beginning the discussion of these matters, we may inquire into the reasons why any person would seek to create a positive impression. What goals are mediated by being judged attractive, and what relationship exists between the particular goal mediated by attraction and the behavior designed to elicit it? It seems useful to distinguish between three major types of goals: *acquisition, protection,* and *signification.* Acquisitive ingratiation perhaps brings us closest to the stereotype of the manipulative, instrumentally oriented, flatterer. The acquisitive case is one in which the target person controls scarce or valuable resources which the ingratiator hopes to acquire at a minimum cost to himself. The ultimate aim, then, is self-benefit: the ingratiator hopes to bias the target person in his favor in order to improve his own outcomes, whether these be provided in terms of salary, a promotion, favorable publicity, expert help and guidance, or a high performance rating. In keeping with the spirit of our definition of ingratiation, this improvement of outcomes is presumed to exceed the level that would normally be available in the course of legitimate social exchange.

In protective ingratiation, the goal is not to improve one's outcomes beyond some otherwise expected level, but rather to prevent or to blunt a potential attack. Protective ingratiation is involved when the individual does not care to reap specific benefits, is not looking for signs of his worth, but cultivates the attraction of others from a motive of foresightful defensive planning. For the protective ingratiator, the world is peopled with potential antagonists, people who can be unkind, hostile, brutally frank. Ingratiation can serve to transform this world into a safer place by depriving the potential antagonist of any pretext for aggression.

An experiment by K. E. Davis and Carolie Florquist, currently in progress, attempts to show that a dependent subordinate will agree more with an irascible, malignant supervisor than with a benign and permissive one. The difference in amount of agreement is reversed when the subordinate is not really dependent on the supervisor's evaluation. The preliminary results of this study appear to confirm this predicted statistical interaction effect.

The goal of protection is probably often sought through self-presentational tactics which concede one's dependence on the target person. The ingratiator, in effect, throws himself on the mercy of the target person, expecting that the norms of reciprocal kindness will protect him from harm. It might be plausibly argued that the transparency of the ingratiator's wish for peace and protection has little bearing on the effectiveness of his tactical behavior. A target person may be attracted to an ingratiator as one is to a defenseless puppy, responding to him with a kind of patronizing nurturance and inhibiting all hostility. At the same time, he may realize that the ingratiator is servile because of his fearful orientation to the world and his lack of resources for coping with any form of aggressive attack.

A final goal mediated by attraction is that of signification. This class of events is distinguished by the fact that attraction is important for what it implies about the worth of the person receiving it. The ulterior benefits which might accrue from creating a positive impression—the increase of interpersonal power implied, or the protection afforded—may be less important to the individual than the fact that approval signifies the value of the recipient, and provides a social definition of his basic lovableness or respectability.

To some extent, these three goals, each of which may be attained through successful attraction-seeking, are probably influenced by individual differences; there may be a crude typology of flatterers: acquisitive manipulators, fearful social isolates, and self-validation seekers. This is likely to be the major justification for distinguishing between acquisition and protection as attraction-mediated goals—while both goals have to do with the balance of outcomes ultimately received by the ingratiator, those who manipulate for special favor are probably rather different in style and in world-view than those who have only self-protection in mind. In a similar vein, those primarily concerned with signification are quite probably insecure and uncertain about their strengths and weaknesses. While there may be merit in pursuing this typological possibility, we wish to emphasize primarily that being judged attractive is not an ultimate goal in interpersonal relations and to raise the question whether the tactics employed in creating a favorable impression are likely to be systematically affected by the individual's underlying purpose.

Before addressing this latter question, however, it may be appropriate to reiterate the distinction between ingratiation and conventions of courtesy which was introduced in chapter one. In addition to the three cases thus far discussed, there is also the broad class of social behaviors which resemble ingratiation but which are normative in their significance rather than designed to elicit attraction. Even to compliment someone who does not objectively merit praise is not necessarily an ingratiating response, if that response is clearly called for by the situation. Ingratiation is often but a subtle or slight extension of the norms of social intercourse. As pointed out in the first chapter, Erving Goffman (1955) has argued that we are all engaged in saving the face of others. We nod agreement with self-enhancing claims that we know to be untrue, we insist that the hostess give us the recipe for a dessert which we actually felt was tasteless and ordinary, and we compliment those who are depressed or insecure about their abilities. In all of these cases we are supporting a general social process and shoring up the fabric of etiquette. We do these things because they are appropriate to the occasion, and if we are well socialized we do them in an almost reflexive and gestural way. *Not* to do them might arouse resentment, but we seek no specific benefit, signal, or protection in return. Though, as indicated above, the same behaviors may be involved in the norms of courtesy as in the case of ingratiation, we are primarily interested in such behaviors when they exploit these norms, and we hope to identify them by remaining especially sensitive to the situations in which the behavior occurs. The distinction between ingratiation and normative face-work is difficult to establish empirically, but it is our conviction that the two can be separated by appropriate steps in an experimental design.

APPROVAL-SEEKING AND SIGNIFICATION

We have said that a person may attempt to create a positive impression so that the signs of approval received may be taken as evidence of his worth as a person. The paradox here is that the greater the ingratiator's efforts to elicit attraction, the less the signifying value of the attraction response. Attraction is relevant to our basic worth only when we have not unduly distorted our characteristics in the attraction-winning attempt. But the paradox may have more logical than psychological validity. It is by no means clear that individuals can readily distinguish between performances which reflect their true self and those which do not. This is clearly implied in the following quotation from Samuel Johnson:

To charge all unmerited praise with the guilt of flattery, and to suppose that the encomiast always knows and feels the falsehoods of his assertions, is surely to discover great ignorance of human nature and human life. In determinations depending not on rules, but on experience and comparison, judgment is always to some degree subject to affection. Very near to admiration is the wish to admire (1779, p. 378).

Goffman (1959) alludes to the problem when he suggests that a performer may either be cynical in projecting an impression for effect or he may be taken in by his own act. Many sociologists who place heavy reliance on the concept of role would be inclined to agree with Cooley (1922) that we train ourselves from the outside inward; that is, the self is erected as a construct which reflects the content of behavior shaped by social expectations. This proposition implies that today's adaptive behavior is part of tomorrow's self, and that the self is undergoing constant revision and momentary fluctuation.

It may be assumed that not all performances are assimilated to the subject's concept of self and that some of his actions have more of a self-revising impact than others. It is a task of social psychology to understand the conditions which favor assimilating versus disowning one's own actions. One important set of conditions concerns the degree of choice which preceded the decision to behave in a certain way, and the consequent degree of personal commitment involved. Festinger's dissonance theory (1957), especially as elaborated by Brehm and Cohen (1962), would unequivocally predict less dissonance if an action at variance with the self-concept were forced on the individual by the environment than if the individual perceived a clear choice between this and more congenial actions. There is abundant evidence that a person's attitudes will change to justify or support unethical actions when the person is induced to perform these actions by subtle cajolery or the promise of minimally sufficient rewards (e.g., Mills, 1958; Davis and Jones, 1960). Festinger and Freedman (1964) argue that certain aspects of value internalization may be explained in terms of dissonance theory.

Thus the parent who threatens mild punishment if a child engages in forbidden behavior will be responsible for greater internalization of the prohibition than one who threatens severe punishment (Aronson and Carlsmith, 1963). The child, in effect, has to provide some of his own justification for not engaging in the behavior, and this may be another way of saying that he internalizes.

If we now return to our concern with ingratiation, it might be argued that conditions which justify the importance of creating a positive impression will lead to ingratiating behavior, but the more dramatic or compelling the justification, the less the person will consider his behavior representative of his "true self." For example, if a person is in a condition of extreme and unusual dependence on someone else, or if he comes from a subculture which values manipulative behavior toward a well-defined class of outsiders, he may be able to engage in ingratiating tactics without its affecting his self-concept in any obvious way. This would be especially true if the tactics he employed were spelled out in detail in something like a salesman's manual. Such occasions must be exceedingly rare in everyday social intercourse, however, and we would expect the ingratiator to confront the problem of potential dissonance arousal in most settings where he sets out to create a positive impression. The broad cultural values of sincerity and of personal consistency in different situations would be to some extent dissonant with the knowledge that one has falsified or distorted one's self-attributes in order to achieve a positive impression.

In pursuing the various ways in which this dissonance might be avoided or reduced, it is important to consider the success of the ingratiation attempt. If a person deliberately sets out to create a positive impression and is rewarded with the approval he tried to obtain, he should be tempted to conclude that his behavior was in fact representative of his normal behavior repertory, that little or no special effort was made to solicit the approval. This should be the case because of the average person's desire to believe the best about himself. Insofar as the ingratiator has any interest in the signifying value of approval, and we assume such an interest may be readily aroused, he will be com-

forted by the belief that the approval represents an endorsement of his true self. Since each person's concept of self is, we
have argued, vague and changeable, we should be able to observe this congenial distortion wherever tactical impression
management is followed by approval.

When a person is given the goal of attempting to create a
favorable impression and is rewarded with disapproval, on the
other hand, he has a readily available explanation for his lack of
success. The disapproval merely serves as evidence of his in-
ability to dissimulate in a convincing manner. If he grasps at
this congenial alternative, we should find him quite ready to an-
nounce that his behavior was not representative and merely reflected a role he was induced to play.

An experiment by Jones, Gergen, and Davis (1962) gathered
evidence bearing on this pair of related hypotheses. Because of
its relevance to the notion of signification, the procedures and
results of that experiment will be described in some detail. Eighty
undergraduate female subjects were individually interviewed under highly controlled conditions by one of ten male graduate
students. For administrative convenience, ten subjects at a time
were interviewed, each being interviewed in a different room.
The subjects were given to believe that the experiment was being
run in conjunction with the "propracticum" course for clinical
psychology trainees. In an initial assembly of each group of
twenty participants, both subjects and interviewers were told,
"We are primarily interested in studying what variables affect
an interviewer's perceptions and evaluations of the person he's
interviewing, and—just as important—what the person being
interviewed thinks of the interviewer."

After this general rationale had been embellished, the interviewers were asked to take an outline of the topics to be covered
in the interview and to seat themselves in the rooms to which
they had been assigned. The subjects were then given further
instructions designed to provide a particular context, or set, for
the interview. All subjects were reminded that the graduate students knew certain instructions were to be given to the subjects,
but that they did not know the nature of these instructions. The
effects of the instructions were presumably to be discussed in

the graduate course they were taking. Half of the subject groups were given the following instructions which were designed to create an *accuracy set:*

Let us suppose that this is an interview designed to help you, and that the interviewer cannot begin to help you unless you are completely honest and accurate about yourself. I don't mean that you should play the part of a neurotic patient or anything like that, but suppose that this is a student counseling interview and that it is very much to your advantage to be completely candid in describing yourself to the interviewer. If you mislead the interviewer, for example, he might end up giving you the wrong advice. One of the problems which always arises in interviews, of course, is that people try to put their best foot forward or, in some cases if an unpleasant job is in the offing, to emphasize their problems and their weak spots. I want you to resist both of these temptations. Just be yourself. Present your self to the interviewer as you actually see yourself and try not to over-emphasize your good points or to play up your failings. Any questions? (Jones, Gergen, & Davis, 1962, p. 5)

would people really be "themselves"?

Subjects in the remaining groups were given instructions designed to create an *ingratiation set*[*]:

Let us suppose that some foundation put up a large sum of money to finance traveling fellowships for a representative group of American college students. Students who qualify for the fellowships will be sent abroad for the summer, to travel around and meet other students in a kind of educational exchange. Let's suppose further that the interviewers are working for this foundation in the southern region and that they will have a large say in whether or not you are considered qualified for one of the fellowships. In such a situation it would naturally be to your advantage to say the kinds of things calculated to make the interviewer think highly of you. This is what I'd like you to do in the coming interview. Try to figure out what kind of person the interviewer probably likes and then try to act like such a person. You can assume that there is no way in which the interviewer can check up on the accuracy of your statements and that you are really quite desperate to be recommended for this fellowship. Try to create the most favorable picture you can, therefore, one which is likely to appeal to the interviewer even though it does not accurately reflect the picture you have of yourself. The only thing you have to remember is that you want to impress the interviewer, but you don't want him to think that you are terribly boastful or unrealistic about yourself. Of course, it is also important that you do not convey to the

[*]Called *hypocrisy set* in the original publication.

interviewer that you are playing some special role. Are there any questions? (pp. 5–6)

During the interview which followed, each interviewer asked the same five questions—primarily designed to support the experimental rationale—and then proceeded to administer orally a Triads Test. Every subject was handed sixteen cards, each of which contained three self-descriptive phrases. These phrases had been preselected to tap different areas of the self-concept such as warmth, tolerance, motivation, activity level, dependability. The three phrases on a particular card referred to one of these areas. One phrase had been judged by several graduate student raters to be a very positive, self-accepting, statement; one had been judged to be slightly self-accepting or slightly belittling but one which most would be willing to endorse as realistic; the final phrase was definitely self-derogating in content. Two examples follow:

A. People invariably find me easy to meet and talk to. (+)
   I am quite active and usually on the go.
   In most respects I am a weak and compliant person. (−)
B. I usually try to be as sincere with others as I can.
   I am basically very impulsive and never stop to think. (−)
   I think I am very well-adjusted in general. (+)

The subject was to examine the phrases on each card and to indicate the one she considered most characteristic of herself, and the one, least characteristic.

From the responses to the Triads Test it was possible to obtain an objective estimate of the subject's tendency to present herself favorably or unfavorably. In a given interview, the subject was given a score of 4 for each item where the positive phrase was designated as most characteristic and the negative phrase as least characteristic. A score of 1 was given for each item where this pattern was reversed. Scores of 2 or 3 were given for intermediate patterns. Thus, by summing the item scores it was possible to compare subjects in the degree of their tendency to choose the most favorable pattern in describing themselves.

Following this interview, the subjects returned to the assembly room and were immediately asked to record their impressions of the interviewer on a twenty-item, Likert-type rating scale. They were then given a (standard and uninformative) brief statement ostensibly outlining the background of the particular interviewer. The only purpose for giving them this information was to provide a pretext for a second impression rating of the interviewer. The subjects then received a statement of feedback indicating the interviewer's impression of them, following which they were given a final opportunity to assess the interviewer by means of the same twenty-item rating scale on which they had previously rated him.

As for the feedback itself, it was actually written by the interviewer (from a standard copy provided beforehand) on a page with the mimeographed heading, Interviewer's Appraisal Sheet. The subject's name was written at the top of the sheet and half of the sheet consisted of a set of mimeographed rating scales which were checked by the interviewer. In the positive feedback condition, the ratings checked were considerably more favorable than those checked in the negative condition. At the bottom of the page, under the mimeographed heading, Overall Impression, the following comments were made in the negative feedback condition:

It is not easy to tell most people what you think of them, but I have been asked to give my honest evaluation, so here goes. Frankly, I would have to say that my impression is not a particularly positive one. By and large I think Miss [the subject's actual name] handles herself quite well and she is generally pleasant and cooperative. But, she seems rather nervous and unsure of herself and the picture she presents on the choice test is quite different from other reactions to this test that we have all seen and discussed in class. From the way she describes herself on those item trios, I honestly don't think I'd care to have her as a friend. I know this sounds blunt, especially since I know she is going to read this. But this is my honest opinion, even though I may be wrong (p. 7).

At the same point on the positive evaluation sheet the following comments were made:

I guess the ratings above speak pretty much for themselves. In my honest opinion, Miss [subject's name] creates a very favorable impression. I don't think I'm just saying this because I know she is going to read this. She is the kind of person I enjoy talking with. She seemed a little ill-at-ease, but no more than one would expect. On the self-concept test, I paid close attention to the things she said about herself. She shows a healthy pattern of attributes. I'm a little embarrassed that there's nothing really to say on the negative side, but that's the way I honestly feel (p. 7).

After recording their "after ratings" of the interviewer, the subjects were interviewed again by a second interviewer, asked to rate him, received approving or disapproving feedback (the opposite of that received after the first interview), and asked to make a second rating. This "replication" feature of the experiment will not be discussed further since the results were quite consistent with reactions to comparable conditions in the first interview. Readers who are interested in changes in self-presentation following approval or disapproval are referred to the more complete report (Jones, Gergen, and Davis, 1962). At the completion of the experiment, each subject filled out a questionnaire designed to tap attitudes toward the experiment, the success of experimental manipulations, and the degree of suspicion aroused. One of the questions asked is of special interest in the present context: the subject was asked to think back to her performance on the Triads Test and to check the percentage of items she felt she answered the way she really saw herself in each of the two interviews.

Turning to the results, we are interested first of all in the impact of instructions on self-presentation and secondly in the impact of approval versus disapproval on the subject's judgment of the representativeness of her own behavior. While the Triads Test probably introduced some elements of artificiality into the interview situation, it also made possible a rather precise measurement of general favorability of self-presentation. It is of incidental interest to note that the Kuder-Richardson reliability coefficient for the Triads Test used in the first interview was .80, indicating that a common factor (presumably level of self-evaluation) pervades responses to the test. As one would expect, subjects in the accuracy set were less positive in their self-evaluations than subjects in the ingratiation set. The possible scoring range was from 16 to 64, the higher the score, the more positive the self-evaluation. Subjects in the ingratiation condition averaged 52.5 while those in the accuracy condition averaged 49.0, a highly significant difference $(p < .01)$. This result is not entirely self-evident; a person might try to impress an interviewer favorably by self-effacing remarks and modest candor. The fact that the ingratiation instructions described a screening interview where an applicant was to be evaluated on personal merit may possibly have contributed to the consistency of self-enhancing responses to the Triads Test. As we shall see below in discussing a study by Gergen (1962), however, the same consistent self-enhancement is noted in response to a different set of instructions to ingratiate—instructions placing a premium on creating a favorable impression, but making no mention of an ulterior goal being mediated by approval.

When asked to evaluate the representativeness of their performance—to indicate the extent to which they had answered in line with their true picture of self—it is not surprising that subjects in the ingratiation condition indicated a significantly lower percentage of self-presentational accuracy than subjects in the accuracy condition $(p < .01)$. After all, subjects in the former condition had been literally invited to play a role and to dissimulate in the line of experimental duty. What is of greater theoretical interest is the fact that the approval versus disapproval variable had a strong effect on the subject's judgments of representativeness and self-validity. There was a highly significant tendency for subjects who received positive feedback to report that their self-presentations were more accurate than did those who received negative feedback $(F = 13.38, p < .001)$. Thus, even though feedback was assigned by a predetermined schedule, following a given interview performance, those subjects receiving approving feedback reported greater accuracy of self-presentation when subsequently questioned. This finding seems more dramatic when one realizes that subjects in the accuracy-disapproval condition reported slightly lower accuracy of self-presentation than subjects in the ingratiation-approval condition.

It seems reasonable to view this latter finding as one bit of experimental evidence supporting the basic proposition that people are eager to believe the best about themselves. When confronted with approving feedback, people will tend to extract from it signifying information concerning their own basic worth, even though they have distorted their self-picture in the attempt to gain this approval.

THE IMPACT OF REINFORCEMENT ON SELF-EVALUATION

While the study by Jones, Gergen, and Davis (1962) provides clear evidence of retrospective distortion, one wonders about the impact of approval on subsequent behavior. Specifically, if a person presents his characteristics in a distorted fashion in order to create the most favorable impression possible, and if he is rewarded with approval after so doing, does this affect in any way what he thinks of himself? This was one of the main questions addressed in a study by Gergen (1962). Once again, female undergraduate subjects were instructed either to present a completely accurate picture of themselves or to create the most favorable impression possible. Throughout their self-presentations, all subjects were reinforced for saying positive things about themselves—the implication being that the reinforcer admired and was attracted to the subject. Gergen predicted that subjects in the ingratiation condition would be more responsive to reinforcement in the process of self-presentation than subjects in the accuracy condition, but that changes in self-presentation which did occur with subjects in the accuracy condition would be more apt to generalize and affect self-esteem ratings in other contexts, or in the presence of a different audience.

There are two alternative reasons why greater generalization effects might be expected under accuracy than under ingratiation instructions. Gergen assumed a two-stage process in the accuracy condition: the approval received should lead to a momentary change in the subject's private view of self, and this should be reflected in the public choice of more favorable attributes as the interview progressed. But the sequence might be reversed: subjects in the accuracy condition might respond to reinforcement with positive changes in public self-presentation which might be followed by accommodation of the private self-concept. Relative to subjects in the accuracy condition, those in the ingratiation treatment would presumably be much more aware of having made a deliberate decision to stretch the truth and, because of this awareness, would be more likely to revert to their prior picture of self after the ingratiation pressure was removed. Those in the accuracy condition who changed their self-presentation in response to approval would reduce the dissonance (attendant on changing their ratings without clear justification) by adapting their private self-image to the change in public presentation of self.

Before examining the results which bear on this general hypothesis, however, let us describe the procedure in greater detail. Fifty-four subjects were interviewed by the same attractive female who, like themselves, was an undergraduate. She was presented as one of a number of juniors and seniors who had been tentatively selected as an interviewer for a large project later in the year. The current session was vaguely described as designed to test interview materials and train the interviewers. Each subject rated herself once prior to the experiment in a classroom setting and again during the interview on a series of seventy-two items similar to those used in the Jones, Gergen, and Davis (1962) study, but more directly derived from the Triads Test developed by Dickoff (1961). The statements on this Self-Valuation Triads (SVT) test covered a wide range of attributes including basic attitudes, values, interests, abilities. Within each item, or triad, one statement reflected a positive trait, one a negative trait, and one a trait more neutral in tone. The favorability of each statement had been established by a group of independent raters and scaled by the Method of Successive Intervals. The instructions for the test required the subject to distribute ten points among the three statements in each triad, so that more points were assigned to the statement considered more self-descriptive and fewer for less applicable statements down to the assignment of zero points if the subject felt that the statement never pertained to her.

As the subject responded orally to the Triads Test during the experimental interview, the interviewer reinforced the subject positively for positive self-ratings and reinforced her negatively when she rated herself negatively. Each triad was typed on a separate card and the cards were handed one at a time to the subject. These cards were arranged so that the subject's initial (classroom) favorability score was approximately the same on each of five blocks of twelve triads. In this manner the baseline score of each subject remained similar from trial block to trial block and there could be no confounding of initial score with trial block position. The interviewer followed elaborate systematic rules in providing reinforcement, but she was carefully trained to appear spontaneous and to vary the specific content of her positive remarks ("Yes, I would agree with. . . ," "Very good." "Yes, I think you are . . .") and her negative remarks ("You don't strike me as being the type who . . . ," "Oh really?" "I sort of disagree with . . ."). As an example of one of the rules followed by the interviewer in assigning positive reinforcement, every time the points assigned to the positive statement equaled or exceeded the subject's previously established average for positive statements, the interviewer would provide positive reinforcement. For purposes of control comparison, eighteen subjects were also interviewed under neutral or nonreinforcing conditions, the interviewer remaining impassive throughout.

After the interview was completed and the interviewer had left, the subject was given twelve additional triads (that is, a sixth block which was also equated for initial level of favorability) and asked to assign points to these as well. The stated rationale for having the subject rate herself on these triads was the need for "normative data," but the experimenter was of course interested in measuring effects of generalization. Following this, the subjects were also asked to fill out a questionnaire designed to measure self-esteem (deCharms and Rosenbaum, 1960). This was a questionnaire that they had also filled out in a pre-experimental classroom session. It provided a more "remote" test of generalization since the items were of a very different format and style than those in the Triads Test.

Half of the subjects in the reinforcement conditions were told prior to the interview that the interviewer's primary task was to be as natural and spontaneous as possible (*personal* condition). The other half were told that the interviewer would merely be practicing interviewing techniques, and that she would not even be able to see the subject during the interview (*impersonal* condition). Subjects in this latter condition were subsequently interviewed in a setting where they could see, but could not be seen by, the stimulus person. We shall defer considering the effects of this variation in personalism until later in this chapter.

Cross-cutting this variation, each subject was assigned one of two different interaction goals or objectives in the interview situation. Subjects in the *accuracy* condition were told:

As far as your behavior is concerned, the most I can say is that as long as you just act naturally and respond to the questions honestly you will have been of great service (Gergen, 1962, p. 115).

Subjects in the *ingratiation* condition were told:

I wonder if you would be willing to try a little experiment. One of the difficulties we are faced with in this project is dealing with the person who isn't so much concerned about being honest when answering the questions, but is primarily trying to make a good impression on our interviewer. There are two things we don't know about in such instances: (a) what kind of picture such a person presents of himself during the interview, that is, how would his answers differ from those of a person who was being totally honest, and (b) how skillful our interviewers are in picking up this kind of thing. So, what I would like to ask you to do while she is interviewing you is to concentrate on only one thing: trying to make the best possible impression on her that you can. I can't tell you how to go about this; this is really what we would like to know. You can say anything you like about yourself, be anybody you would like to be, just as long as you think your answers will impress her . . . (p. 117).

Turning to the results, we may first examine the differential impact of these instructions to be accurate or ingratiating on self-presentation during the interview itself. Figure 1 presents the average difference by experimental condition between each subject's level of self-evaluation in the "neutral" classroom situation and his level of self-evaluation on the same items during the experiment. The vertical axis therefore represents the degree to which subjects assigned more points to the positive statement of each item triad in the experimental than in the classroom situation. As Figure 1 indicates, the interviewer's reinforcing activities were effective in raising the favorability of self-presentation. Not only did the average reinforced subject present herself

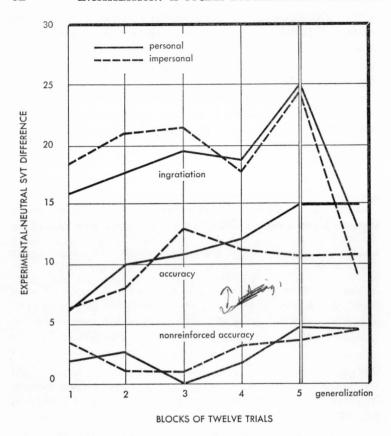

FIGURE 1——Mean SVT experimental-neutral difference scores across blocks of trials for all conditions

more positively in the experimental than in the classroom situation ($F = 27.95, p < .001$), but subjects in the reinforced accuracy conditions were significantly more self-enhancing than those control subjects who were not reinforced ($F = 14.46, p < .001$). As Figure 1 shows, all of the nonreinforced subjects were operating under accuracy instructions—half with a personal and half with an impersonal interviewer. There was no comparable control for subjects in the ingratiation condition.

It is also very evident from Figure 1 that subjects in the ingratiation conditions were more self-enhancing than those in the accuracy condition ($F = 19.36, p < .001$). There were, however, no differences between the two conditions as a function of trial blocks, though the overall upward trend was significant for all reinforced subjects taken together ($F = 6.08, p < .025$). As Figure 1 suggests, and as a detailed examination of self-presentation during the first trial block confirms, subjects in the ingratiation conditions start out assigning more points to the positive statement of the triads, and maintain their greater self-enhancement throughout the interview. These results serve to replicate the findings of the Jones, Gergen, and Davis (1962) experiment reported above: when told to make a favorable impression on an interviewer, female subjects responded to this task by exaggerating their strengths and minimizing their weaknesses. The results do not show, however, that subjects in the ingratiation conditions were more sensitive to reinforcement than subjects in the accuracy conditions. In fact, the significant overall effect of trial blocks is more a consequence of cumulative shifts in the accuracy than in the ingratiation conditions. An interesting follow-up to the present study would involve the reinforcement of modesty and self-deprecation, though there would be some peculiar problems involved in preventing the subject's psychological or even physical withdrawal from the situation in such a treatment. The reinforcer would have to convince the subject that he liked the latter because of his (reinforced) modesty, not that he found the subject unimpressive relative to others.

In the context of our present interest in the significance of approval, we wish to take special note of the generalization of self-presentational changes. Is there any evidence that the public self-enhancement produced by the reinforcing interviewer has an impact on the average subject's private self-assessment? Do the results confirm the finding in the Jones, Gergen, and Davis (1962) study that, even after being specifically instructed to indulge in the hypocritical arts of ingratiation, subjects treated resulting approval as providing valid information about the self? Figure 1 shows that there were striking differences in the generalization value of reinforcement as a function of prior instructional set. Subjects in the ingratiation conditions showed a sharp decline in the favorability of self-description when asked to respond to a final block of twelve trials after the interviewer had left. Subjects in the accuracy conditions, on the other hand, maintained the positive level of self-appraisal which their responses had reached by the fifth reinforced block. The loss in favorability of self-evaluation from the fifth learning block to the generalization block was, as predicted, significantly greater in the ingratiation conditions than in the accuracy conditions ($p < .001$). Such a finding seems to accord clearly with common sense. Since the instructional pressure to be ingratiating was responsible for the highly positive fifth block scores, removal of this pressure should result in a severe decrease in favorability of self-evaluation.

But there is another way of viewing Figure 1 and considering the effects of generalization. This is to ignore the actual amount of decrease from the fifth trial block and to concentrate instead on the "generalization gain" as measured against the base line of the response to these items in the prior classroom setting. Here a fact of both practical and theoretical significance is that subjects in the ingratiation conditions ended up with roughly the same enhanced view of themselves as did those in the accuracy conditions. Reinforced subjects in general had higher scores on the generalization triads than on the same triads under the neutral conditions ($p < .01$), and there were no significant differences among treatment groups. As Figure 1 suggests, subjects in the nonreinforced groups showed somewhat higher self-ratings on the generalization triads than they did in the neutral testing session, though the differences here did not approach significance.

A more subtle test of generalization effects was made possible by the readministration of the deCharms-Rosenbaum self-esteem scale after the interview and the generalization triads. Table 1 presents the mean for each group under neutral and post-experimental conditions. An analysis of variance of the self-

TABLE 1——Means and standard deviations of de-Charms-Rosenbaum self-esteem scores obtained in the pre-experimental and post-experimental testing sessions

| | | ACCURACY | | INGRATIATION | |
		PRE-EXPERI-MENTAL	POST-EXPERI-MENTAL	PRE-EXPERI-MENTAL	POST-EXPERI-MENTAL
REINFORCED PERSONAL	MEAN	45.22	50.78	43.77	51.44
	SD	5.85	6.53	8.76	8.25
REINFORCED IMPERSONAL	MEAN	46.88	50.66	47.00	50.88
	SD	6.54	7.11	8.94	9.75
NONREINFORCED PERSONAL	MEAN	42.55	47.88		
	SD	10.44	10.86		
NONREINFORCED IMPERSONAL	MEAN	45.55	46.44		
	SD	7.08	9.03		

esteem scores of the reinforced groups, comparing neutral with post-experimental scores, indicates that the post-experimental scores were significantly higher ($p < .01$). It should be noted that a considerable shift took place in the nonreinforced personal condition. An analysis of variance of the nonreinforced groups only did not yield any significant differences, but the difference between reinforced and nonreinforced subjects in the accuracy conditions was not significant.

While the evidence concerning the role of reinforcement in producing generalization on the self-esteem scale is not entirely convincing because of the unexpected shift in the nonreinforced personal condition, the overall picture of post-experimental self-enhancement is striking. Of special interest is the fact that subjects in the ingratiation conditions, like those in the accuracy conditions, ended up describing themselves more positively after the reinforcing interview. At least on the dimension of self-evaluation, then, the immediate impact of the receipt of reinforcement for saying more positive things about oneself was roughly the same in both accuracy and ingratiation conditions. Perhaps it is not too meaningful to compare the conditions, however, since in line with the rules governing reinforcement procedures, the average subject received more approval in the ingratiation than in the accuracy condition.

It is unfortunate that because of the limited supply of available subjects there was not a condition where ingratiation instructions were followed by a nonreinforcing interview. Since the completion of the initial study, however, enough additional subjects *were* run in this condition to make it quite clear that the reinforcement received was important to the generalization effect. Gergen reports (personal communication) that ingratiation instructions, in the absence of subsequent reinforcement, do not result in high self-ratings on the generalization triads or on the self-esteem scale.

In addition to these data recently gathered by Gergen, both the results of the Jones, Gergen, and Davis (1962) experiment and the evidence of low and nonsignificant generalization in the nonreinforced accuracy groups support the contention that the approval implied by reinforcement was an important factor in the ingratiation conditions. The typical subject in this condition engaged in exaggerated self-enhancement during the interview, and the more she stressed her positive attributes, the more reinforcement and agreement she received. While she could not deny to herself that she had put forth an idealized version of her characteristics, when asked to revert to her normal self she was inclined to stretch the picture in her favor. Such a change could be easily rationalized since an even more favorable self-presentation was consistenly supported by an attractive peer in the recent past. Therefore, the subject in the ingratiation conditions could gain the pleasures of self-enchancement in filling out the generalization triads without having to acknowledge a lack of candor to herself or to the experimenter.

An issue which is relevant to the question of attaching personal significance to approval is the extent to which the subjects were aware of misrepresenting their characteristics during the course of the interview. All subjects were asked immediately after the neutral testing session and again after the experimental interview, how truly representative they felt their ratings were, and how confident they were in the stability of these ratings. Since the answers to these questions were highly correlated at both times, each subject was assigned a "felt sincerity" score by combining the ratings on both items. Subjects in the ingratiation conditions felt that they were significantly less sincere in the experimental situation than in the neutral testing period (p < .001). Since all subjects in these conditions received approving reinforcement, any contributions of this latter variable cannot be assessed. In keeping with the results of the Jones, Gergen, and Davis (1962) experiment, one would expect that the decrease in felt sincerity would have been even greater in the absence of reinforcing approval. Subjects in each of the accuracy conditions, on the other hand, felt that they were more sincere—that their self-presentation was more representative—in the experimental than in the neutral situation. This was as true for the nonreinforced subjects as for those in the reinforced-accuracy conditions (though the change was not significant for the accuracy-impersonal subjects). Apparently the accuracy instructions either had a direct effect on subsequent claims of sincerity, or they in fact induced greater care in responding to the triads. As one subject put it, "In the [neutral testing session] I went through pretty fast, without paying a whole lot of attention; today I spent more time on each [triad] and studied them more carefully."

We have taken the position that persons tend to exaggerate the perceived representativeness or felt sincerity of any performance which elicits approval. The felt sincerity ratings in Gergen's (1962) experiment appear to reflect pre-experimental instructions rather than autistic distortion in response to approval, though we have already noted that approval was a constant in the ingratiation conditions and its effects cannot be assessed. Some support for the original argument of congenial self-deception may be salvaged, however, if it is realized that (as measured from their own pre-experimental base line) subjects in the accuracy-reinforced conditions did in fact misrepresent themselves more than subjects in the accuracy-nonreinforced conditions. Especially in the reinforced accuracy personal condition, there is a linear trend ($p < .01$) in the direction of increasing favorability of self-rating throughout the interview. It would be difficult to argue that such a trend reflects accuracy, especially in view of the careful prearrangement of item position to avoid precisely this kind of confounding. Thus the data support the notion that reinforced subjects in the accuracy personal condition are considerably less accurate than their nonreinforced controls while claiming equal, high accuracy on the felt sincerity measure.

This argument would be more plausible if there were some clear reason why more distortion should be expected in the reinforced accuracy personal condition than in any other condition. Since this was the only condition in which a significant increase across blocks was observed, it is the only condition in which changes in self-presentation are clearly related to the interviewer's reinforcements. If we were to inquire into the condition in which approval would logically have the greatest significance for one's appraisal of one's own worth, the accuracy personal condition would surely be the one. Not only is the subject consciously trying to be honest in presenting her true self in this condition, but the interviewer is presumably attuned to the subject's background, her appearance, and her idiosyncratic strengths and weaknesses. For these reasons, perhaps, it is important for subjects in this condition to insist that they have been accurate even though their self-presentation has obviously been affected by recurrent signs of approval. Subjects in the reinforced accuracy impersonal condition are somewhat less affected by reinforcement itself (the linear trend for trial blocks is not quite significant in their case) and somewhat less inclined to emphasize how sincere they were during the interview. Of all of the groups originally receiving accuracy instructions, the reinforced accuracy impersonal group was the only one which did not show a significant increase in felt sincerity when going from the neutral to the experimental session.

Another aspect of awareness is the extent to which subjects

acknowledged that they were more positive during the interview than in the neutral session and *also* felt that the positive attitude of the interviewer had a positive effect on their self-ratings. It is extremely interesting to note that only those subjects who *denied* being influenced by the interviewer in the accuracy conditions actually manifested any learning—in the sense of increasing the favorability of self-presentation from block to block. This trend was stronger in the personal than in the impersonal variation of the accuracy conditions, though very few subjects were involved when the comparison reached that level of refinement. The finding that the more aware the accuracy subject is, the less he learns, suggests that only those subjects who at some point resist the influence of the interviewer are later willing to acknowledge that they were influenced by her. Such a finding is clearly in keeping with the notion that one should not modify one's self-presentation to gain more approval when instructed to be accurate and honest. Those who do modify their presentations must convince themselves, the experimenter, or both, that they have not done so. The fact that this defensive distortion enables the affected subject to believe in the validity of her enhanced self is, of course, compatible with the main argument of this chapter.

In contrast, it might also be pointed out that those subjects in the ingratiation condition who expressed some awareness of "stressing what she seemed to approve" showed a higher over-all level of self-evaluation during the interview. This is hardly surprising, especially since any subject who hypothesized that a positive impression could best be achieved by self-enhancement would (a) have a more favorable self-presentation score and also (b) receive more confirmatory reinforcement. The awareness data for the subjects in the ingratiation conditions are primarily of interest because of the contrast they provide with subjects in the accuracy conditions. In fact, the statistical interaction implied by the discussion above—aware subjects having higher scores in the ingratiation conditions and lower scores in the accuracy conditions—becomes larger block by block until it is significant on the fifth and last block of trials.

To summarize the major effects of the variation in instructions to be ingratiating versus accurate, Gergen's results showed a striking over-all effect on favorability of self-presentation, with subjects in the ingratiation conditions being generally much more self-enhancing. While the general trend of all reinforced conditions was toward greater favorability as the experimental interview progressed, only in the accuracy personal condition did this trend become significant. Subjects in the ingratiation condition showed a significantly greater generalization decrease than subjects in the accuracy conditions (who, on the average, showed little or none). Ingratiation subjects, nevertheless, rated themselves higher on post-experimental "neutral" triads than they did in the previous classroom condition. In this respect reinforcement of positive statements about the self had comparable residual effects regardless of the obvious differences between the motivational orientations of subjects in the ingratiation versus accuracy conditions. Such a finding was considered circumstantial, but not conclusive, evidence of the average person's willingness to believe the best about himself. Further evidence from the data on awareness was adduced to support this interpretation, though subjects in the ingratiation conditions were well aware that they had falsified their presentation of self during the interview. Among subjects in the accuracy conditions, those who showed the greatest increase in favorability were the ones most likely to emphasize the accuracy of their performance and to deny being affected by the interviewer's reinforcements.

The Target Person's Vanity
and the Success of Ingratiation

The most salient and intriguing characteristic of ingratiation, or at least of acquisitive ingratiation, is that social influence is being implicitly sought while being explicitly denied by the actor. The behavior in question is not only designed to produce an effect on the target person, but the whole attempt involves a more or less illegitimate social exchange. Partly because of the illegitimacy of exchange, and partly because of a built-in resistance to influence attempts which are not based on greater access to information or on readily conceded expertise, the target person is likely to succumb to the actor's blandishments the more obviously these reflect the manipulative intent (that is, the self-interest) of the actor.

In most settings of social interaction, the same range of cues defining the setting are available to each participant. While there are, of course, small or large differences in perspective, the more important fact is that of cognitive overlap and agreement concerning the structure of the situation and its motive-arousing features. Concretely, if participant A has substantially greater resources than participant B, both are usually aware of this fact and it is one which inevitably colors their relationship. In such a situation we would say that B is potentially dependent on A, or that A has power over B because he can give or withold important benefits from his ample supply. Our present interest is in the cognitive side of such a relationship. Because the actor, B, has much to gain by successfully ingratiating himself with A, the same features of the situation which lead B to conceal his manipulative motives should alert A to the motivational possibilities reflected in B's behavior. Thus it might appear that, given a common understanding of a situation and the psychological positions it creates, each ingratiation attempt should be confronted by a defense against providing precisely the type of benefit ingratiation is designed to secure. This leaves one with the curious conclusion that ingratiation is most likely to work—to elicit attraction—when that attraction is relatively valueless and when no obvious benefits are involved.

This conclusion is probably valid, other things being equal, but in the case of social interaction they rarely are. For one thing, while we have stressed the common availability of cues defining the situation, there are occasions when these cues are not equally available to each participant in the interaction or, at least, are differentially perceived by them. In fact, it would seem important to the ingratiator to conceal or disguise his dependence condition, and thus to slip by the defenses which would normally be erected by the target person. Even if we assume a shared understanding of situational dynamics, however, other factors must be carefully considered in predicting the fate of an ingratiation attempt.

One of these factors is the almost unique ambiguity of just those kinds of behavior likely to be involved in ingratiation. Compliments and conformity, for the most part, are extremely unreliable indicators of motivational intent. As indicated above, precisely the same behavior may be devious and instrumental, a casual concession to the norms of courtesy, a pathetic defensive move, or even, of course, a perfectly honest and ingenuous expression of belief. There is little in the behavior itself which helps the perceiver identify underlying motives. Derogatory and disagreeable remarks typically carry their own motivational implications; supportive and agreeable ones are difficult to interpret without careful appraisal of their surrounding situational context.

Even if the supportive and agreeable remarks are delivered in a context which is rich in cues implying ulterior motivation, the actor's dependence, or his engagement in ritual courtesy and face-work, there is no guarantee that these cues will be properly evaluated by the target person. We have already argued that the ingratiator is quite willing to believe the best of himself, and we have presented evidence indicating the extent to which he may exaggerate his self-presentational candor after giving a distorted view of his characteristics in order to gain approval. This desire to believe the best about ourselves is a reflection of what we may call vanity. While variations in self-esteem and other personal attributes undoubtedly underlie variations in the level of vanity as an individual characteristic, none of us is immune to vanity's infectious encroachments. This means, of course, that vanity not only underlies the ingratiator's self-deceptions, but also conditions the susceptibility of the target person to the tactical blandishments of others. "Every man willingly gives value to the praise which he receives and considers the sentence passed in his favor as a sentence of discernment" (Johnson, 1779, p. 378).

We shall have more to say in chapter seven about the range of factors involved in predicting the target person's response to ingratiating overtures, but certain evidence from the Gergen (1962) study serves to dramatize the role that vanity may play in a person's response to approval. While we have to this point treated the subjects in that experiment as involved in more or less ingratiating self-presentations, it is also possible to view the subjects as targets of the reinforcing interviewer's persistent compliments. Of special significance in this context is the personalism variable, about which little has thus far been said. The experiment was originally designed to explore the cross-cutting effects of dramatic differences in the subjects' motivations during the interview and equally dramatic differences in the perceived role of the interviewer, while holding constant the latter's actual behavior. Gergen predicted that reinforcement from the personal interviewer would be more effective in influencing the subject's self-image than reinforcement from the impersonal interviewer, and that this would be revealed by self-presentational changes during the interview and greater generalization effects subsequently. We have noted that the personalism variable contributed to the magnitude of certain effects under accuracy instructions, and that certain predicted relationships were significant in the accuracy personal condition which were not significant in the accuracy impersonal condition. However, at no point were there any clearly significant differences as a function of variations in personalism. To interpret this basically negative result, it is especially important to present the procedures creating the variation in greater detail.

In both the personal and the impersonal conditions, the subjects were told that the interview was a kind of training session for the interviewer and a pre-test for the interview materials. In the *personal* conditions, however, the subjects were then told:

Actually, the one thing which stands out about these training sessions is that the interviewers have almost no instructions. Their task is first and foremost to get to know the person interviewed as well as possible during the time they have. To do this we felt we couldn't impose a lot of restrictions on them as far as how they should act with different people—that is, we didn't want to send out a group of people who would just be giving ready-made performances. It's amazing how quick people are to pick up this kind of superficiality. Instead, we wanted the interviewers to be able to give full concentration to the person whom they were dealing with, rather than worrying about how they appeared or about the front they were putting up. . . . [Therefore we have given the interviewer] as few instructions as possible—just enough so that she knows how to use the materials. . . . As far as her job is concerned, she has the real difficult task of having to put together as much information about a person as she can in a short time period and trying to formulate her own ideas about the person on the basis of this information. This means she has to be as open as possible to information about others, considering each as an individual . . . (Gergen, 1962, pp. 114–115).

In addition to these instructions, subjects in the personal condition were introduced to the interviewer who remained in the room while the experimenter asked several questions of the subject. These questions inquired about her hometown, her father's occupation, and her dating status. The subject was finally asked to recount an incident of which she was proud and another incident about which she was embarrassed. The interviewer then left the room, presumably to record her first impression of the subject. In several minutes she returned to conduct the interview face to face with the subject.

In effect, every effort was made to emphasize the spontaneity of the interview in the personal conditions and to make the subject feel that the interviewer was responding to her as an individual, taking into account both her appearance, her manner, and her answers to the experimenter's questions. In contrast, subjects in the *impersonal* conditions were told:

Each of the interviewers has been through some pretty intensive training sessions where she was instructed in how an interviewer should act, what kinds of things she should say, how she would build up rapport between herself and the person being interviewed, and that sort of thing. The point here was to make sure that each interviewer's behavior was pretty much standard. (You can imagine what the results would be if we let each interviewer go around acting in her own personal way.) . . . by now they seem to have a pretty good understanding of proper interviewing techniques and rules for their behavior, but they just need some practice in putting these techniques to use (Gergen, 1962, pp. 115–116).

In addition to these instructions concerning the interviewer's orientation to the task, the interviewer never met the subject and was never exposed to any information about her other than that eventually contained in the subject's response to the Triads Test and to three warm-up questions always asked by the interviewer (concerning year in school, most likely major, and spare time activities). The experimenter asked the same questions about background prior to the interview, but it was made clear that the subject's answers would not be made available to the interviewer. The interview was actually conducted with the subject and interviewer separated by a one-way mirror. It was carefully explained to the subject that she could see the interviewer but could not be seen by her (which, in fact, was true). The interview was conducted over a microphonic sound system.

Given the confines of a laboratory situation and the necessity of standardizing the actual responses of the interviewer, it is hard to imagine a more extreme variation in the interpersonal context in which reinforcement is delivered. In the impersonal conditions, obvious pains were taken to deprive the reinforcement of its signification value and to make it difficult for the subject to conclude with confidence that she, personally, was found attractive by the interviewer. And yet, a striking thing about the self-presentation results summarized in Figure 1 is the similarity of learning and generalization curves for comparable personal and impersonal conditions. Figure 1 does reveal a suggestive tendency for the curve to level off in the accuracy impersonal condition, but the difference between the two accuracy conditions does not approach significance.

Negative results always present special difficulties in interpretation since their meaning depends so heavily on the validity of independent variable manipulations and on the sensitivity of dependent variable measures. In the present case the impact of the personalism variation may have been blunted by the vanity of the average subject who was reinforced or given approval. A measure of perceived personalism was included on the post-experimental questionnaire. This consisted of combining the subject's responses to two questions, "To what extent did you feel the interviewer was acting naturally and spontaneously?" and "To what extent did the interviewer seem bound to a set of rules governing her behavior during the interview?" Subjects in the impersonal conditions were significantly more reluctant than those in the personal conditions to answer the first question in the affirmative and the second in the negative ($p < .01$ in both cases). Apparently the subjects' desire to believe that the approval was genuine did not completely override the personalism variation on questions directly geared to the manipulation and its immediate implications for interviewer behavior. However, subjects were also asked to predict on a series of evaluative traits the interviewer's true feelings about them after the interview. Since this task was a more indirect reflection of the personalism variation, we might expect to find greater distortion in the service of vanity. Specifically, subjects should want to believe that the interviewer thought highly of them and in this way to increase the perceived signification value of approval received.

This expectation can be checked by combining the prediction ratings into a score reflecting the judged favorability of the interviewer's impression of the subject. Table 2 presents the means and standard deviations of scores on this combined cluster of evaluative traits. The main evidence for vain distortion in this table is the high predicted evaluation in the accuracy impersonal condition. The mean score in the ingratiation impersonal con-

TABLE 2——Means and standard deviations of predictions of the stimulus person's ratings on the combined evaluative cluster*

		ACCURACY	INGRATIATION
REINFORCED PERSONAL	MEAN	78.21	81.66
	SD	8.64	8.86
REINFORCED IMPERSONAL	MEAN	80.21	71.22
	SD	6.85	12.74

* Note—The higher the mean, the more positive the predicted evaluation.

dition is significantly lower than the ingratiation personal condition mean ($p < .05$) and almost significantly lower than the accuracy impersonal mean. Apparently the combination of instructions to ingratiate and the emphasis on impersonality of approving feedback is sufficient to inhibit the tendency to assume that the approving remarks reflect a genuinely positive appraisal. It should be remembered that subjects in the ingratiation conditions received much more positive feedback than those in the accuracy conditions, making it difficult to accept the credibility of approval indicators—especially when this credibility has been undermined by instructions creating the impersonal context. On the other hand, in spite of the dramatic difference between personal and impersonal contexts, subjects in the accuracy impersonal condition are quite willing to believe that the interviewer genuinely likes and admires them. In the two nonreinforced accuracy conditions variations in personalism have no effect, and the level of predicted favorability is approximately as low as the level in the ingratiation impersonal condition.

These results give support to the notion of vain distortion, but they also suggest conditions under which the reality constraints are too great for distortion to occur. If the individual is deliberately trying to create a positive impression or to be ingratiating, and if he is forewarned that he himself might be the target of ingratiation to establish rapport, little signification value is attached to the approval received. On the other hand, signs of approval tend to be accepted at face value when these particular conditions do not occur in combination. The ingratiator presumably considers the approval genuine in a personal context, and the person who is trying to be accurate considers the approval genuine regardless of strong evidence that it may be perfunctory and based on specified role prescriptions.

SUMMARY AND CONCLUSIONS

It has been the purpose of this chapter to emphasize the role of autistic distortion in the ingratiation episode. We have presented evidence from one experiment indicating that ingratiators who succeed in their efforts to gain approval, tend to recall their self-presentations as more accurate than those who do not succeed—even though their responses are equally false and equally self-enhancing. Findings from a second experiment suggest that subjects who present themselves amidst recurrent approval from an attractive peer show at least a temporary increase in generalized self-esteem. The pre-experimental to post-experimental shift is approximately as great whether the preceding performance of the subject was originally designed to be ingratiating or to be accurate. Both sets of findings may be interpreted as reflecting the normal human desire to treat approval from others as a signal of basic personal worth, even though the behavior eliciting approval has been colored by such tactical considerations as concealing or minimizing negative self-attributes. The relative ambiguity of one's self-concept, and one's pervasive uncertainty concerning where one stands on most evaluative dimensions, make this kind of retrospective distortion possible. Vanity, the wish to believe the best of oneself, provides direction to the distortion. When one is approved of, one's basic self has been glimpsed and admired. When one receives disapproving feedback, one is reluctant to accept this as evidence about one's true character and one readily entertains other hypotheses.

The ease with which one can distort the relationship between one's self-revealing acts and one's private self-conception is an important reason for the ubiquitousness of ingratiation. In spite of the shady ethical status of effect-oriented behavior, the individual can afford, with the help of the kinds of convenient self-deceptions described in this chapter, to engage in such tactics without flagrantly violating his conscience. In providing evidence that acts greeted with approval are viewed by the actor as genuinely self-reflecting, we add support to Goffman's statement that one can be taken in by one's own performance. Moreover, we have specified one of the theoretically reasonable conditions, the receipt of approval, under which this phenomenon is most likely to occur. An interesting methodological implication is that even the most candid subject may find it impossible, in response to a post-experimental query, to distinguish between dissimulation and realistic self-presentation as long as approval or disapproval are clearly involved. Because the individual is victimized by his own vanity, his responses to such questions cannot be accepted as indicative of his own motives in launching an action sequence.

Looking at the ingratiation episode from the vantage point of the target person, we argued that the motivational intent underlying received approval may similarly be distorted in the service of the target person's vanity. The individual who receives flattering approval is generally inclined to believe that the approval is sincere and not a product of dissimulation or strategic role-playing. We have presented evidence to support this additional argument concerning human fallibility, but we have also noted certain limiting conditions on the vanity-distortion hypothesis. If a person's self-presenting actions are preceded by instructions urging him to be accurate, he will tend to view the subsequent approval of another as heartfelt in spite of elaborate contextual arrangements designed to convince the subject that the approval is merely part of an impersonal social ritual. The ritual basis for the approval is apparently conceded, however, if the person is impersonally approved following his attempt to act on instructions to be ingratiating.

A somewhat different side of the general vanity-distortion argument, a side the grounds for which are yet to be demonstrated, is that subjects engaged in flattery or other-enhancement should be motivated to believe in the validity of their own compliments. It thus appears that both the ingratiator and the target person are anxious to believe that the latter is better than he really is. There is, then, a kind of unwitting autistic conspiracy involved in much of human intercourse. Compliments designed for effect become construed by both the flatterer and the target person as valid appraisals, and the informational value of evaluative communications is blurred or distorted at both ends of the channel. This is not the last we shall hear of this unwitting conspiracy, for the complexities of autistic distortion are a common feature of most of the experiments to come. Before proceeding to these further studies, however, we shall attempt systematically to analyze the ingratiation episode. After the cognitive and motivational dynamics of the ingratiator have been identified more explicitly, we will be in a more favorable position to make predictions concerning the vicissitudes of tactical behavior.

4 Cognitive and Motivational Determinants of Acquisitive Ingratiation

To the extent that ingratiation may be distinguished from other forms of socially responsive behavior, it becomes pertinent to attempt a systematic analysis of the circumstances giving rise to this attraction-oriented cluster of responses. When does a person make a special effort to be agreeable, complimentary, or personally appealing in an effort to gain attraction? How is the form of this effort—its tactical nature—affected by the specific conditions of the social interchange we are studying?

In order to pursue this analysis in some detail, it is useful to introduce a simple notational system patterned after Heider's (1946) skeletal terminology of "naive" psychology. While creating an attractive impression is the immediate goal of the ingratiator, in general the phenomena we are discussing fall under the heading of benefits given and received. The benefits may be quite specific in nature (a raise in pay, cancellation of a traffic ticket) or quite general (favored treatment in unknown future contingencies). An act of flattery or ingratiation is one in which p causes x in o's presence, acting on the assumption that o likes, needs, will appreciate, or will feel grateful for x. In the typical acquisitive case, x is designed ultimately to instigate or arouse o

to produce y, a benefit desired by p. As indicated above, p may not be completely aware of the purchase relationship involved in his production of x to receive y. In order for the desired exchange to be effected, a number of conditions must be present: o must in fact desire, like, or appreciate x; he must in fact be capable of producing y; and he must feel in some way that y is the appropriate response to x, that y is the right kind of reaction to a person who gives x.

In the following discussion, p always stands for the potential ingratiator, x for a definable molar unit of his behavior, o for the recipient of this behavior, and y for the benefit controlled by o and desired by p. We shall not be strict in assigning a meaning to y; therefore sometimes it will stand for signs of approval and at other times y shall stand for the concrete benefits mediated by approval. We will also find a use for the symbol z, to stand for disapproval and for responses under o's control which would harm p or be negative for him.

1. INCENTIVE-BASED DETERMINANTS

Ingratiation is motivated behavior directed toward the goal of eliciting increased attraction from a particular person. While some specific benefit may be sought, by our definition it is sought by the ingratiator through the mediation of increased attraction. The power of this goal to arouse or instigate ingratiation should be a direct function of the following variables: (a) the importance or value of y to p, (b) the perceived uniqueness of o as a source of y, and (c) o's perceived ability and disposition to produce negatively valued zs.

Turning first to the *importance of y to p*, one can specify a number of conditions which enhance the importance or value of attraction or approval. Some of these conditions are undoubtedly dispositional: because of his personal motivational structure or self-concept, p brings into the average social situation a strong need to be loved, approved, or admired. One can imagine some of the individual differences which might correlate with such a disposition: stability of self-esteem, need for affiliation, strength of dependency needs, fear of aggression and rejection. In the study by Jones, Gergen, and Davis (1962), which exposed female subjects to positive and negative evaluations of themselves, it was found that those who scored high on Christie's Mach Scale (a measure based on the endorsement of Machiavellian sentiments and described in Christie and Merton, 1958) were—relative to low-scorers—unresponsive to feedback from others. A content analysis of free self-descriptions in this experiment showed that the dimension of Machiavellianism, or cynicism, is closely related to other-directedness versus inner-directedness (Riesman, 1950), so that inner-directedness, endorsement of cynical or Machiavellian statements, and seeming unresponsiveness to the expressed evaluations of another seem to form a cluster. It is not clear exactly how responsiveness to evaluative feedback is related to the tendency to engage readily in ingratiating overtures, but such responsiveness suggests itself as an index of the general importance of social approval which, theoretically, should be one of the component motivational factors underlying ingratiation.

There is considerable additional evidence that self-esteem is an important variable in determining one's responsiveness to feedback from others. The general conclusion that one might draw from studies by Jones, Hester, Farina, and Davis (1959), deCharms and Rosenbaum (1960), Rosenbaum and deCharms (1960), and Cohen (1959) is that persons low in self-esteem become more desperately involved in any situation having implications of social evaluation and are more responsive to feedback about themselves. A correlational finding in Gergen's (1962) experiment, the major results of which were described in the last chapter, adds further support to this proposition. The lower the subject's initial self-esteem, the more responsive she was to recurrent approval in increasing the favorability of her self-presentation. Interestingly enough, low self-esteem was also associated with maintaining the level of favorability on a generalization test. This seems to be evidence of the greater impact of approval on the subject's view of self. We would expect the same subject to decrease the favorability of her self-presentation in the face of disapproval since in general she should tend to reflect with little resistance the surrounding context of appraisal.

In addition to dispositional factors, there are obviously situational conditions which increase or decrease the importance of social approval. Some of these are simply the transient or momentary coordinates of the dispositional variables discussed above. For example, an individual who has just been criticized or belittled in a convincing way may have his needs for positive social feedback aroused because of his momentarily lowered self-esteem. One can imagine the value of y fluctuating, then, as a function of success and failure experiences in the immediate past. As we have noted in chapter two, there are complicated issues involved here, and we have to contend with Deutsch and Solomon's (1959) evidence that a person who has failed responds less positively to someone who subsequently praises her than does a person who has succeeded. As mentioned earlier, credibility may be a crucial factor here and highly credible support would be especially appreciated after failure.

Related to the conditions of failure or belittlement is the condition of social deprivation. If the individual has been deprived of social contact in the immediate past, he may be more grateful for, and therefore responsive to, approval. Gewirtz and Baer (1958), for example, found that children were more affected by verbal approval (they showed greater improvement in performance) if they had previously been exposed to twenty minutes of social isolation than if not so exposed. There is a strong analogical basis here for arguing that an individual's need for approval may be aroused by prior conditions of social isolation, though the contingency may be a fragile one and subject to many other influences.

The preceding examples have involved the equation of y with direct signs of approval and attraction. If y is allowed to stand for a more concrete and specific benefit controlled by o, the conditions which might determine the value of this benefit to p are diverse, numerous, and in many cases easy to measure or to manipulate. In one case y might stand for the size of a merit bonus at the disposal of a supervisor. In another case, y might signify the attractiveness of a professional position sought by p

and controlled by o. One might even imagine the extreme case where y might stand for life versus death. The defendant in a murder trial is dependent on the judge's control of this critical y, and so to a lesser extent the American soldiers imprisoned in North Korean camps were dependent on their captors. The importance of y to p is clearly a critical feature of the power that o has over p, a consideration which will receive considerable attention in chapter five.

Arousing a motive to be ingratiating is critically, but not exclusively, dependent on the value of y that o can provide. It is also important to consider the *uniqueness of* o *as a source of* y. P may have powerful needs for approval but o may be one among many available sources of approval. It may be stated as a testable, but not self-evident, proposition that the strength of the motive to be ingratiating to a particular o varies inversely with the number and saliency of other os who can also produce a valued y. This would seem to be a reasonable proposition if only because p is likely to assume that at least one of the available os will probably produce y for his consumption in the absence of the risky x, ingratiating behavior. A further implication of the conditions where many os can mediate y is that p's relative dependence is reduced or his power enhanced. If o derives any rewards from keeping p in the relationship, at least, he will be more responsive to p's wishes to the extent that p can threaten to go elsewhere for his ys (cf. Thibaut and Kelley's, 1959, discussion of comparison level for alternatives). As a dramatic example of the relationship between o's uniqueness as a "gatekeeper" of y and p's motivation to be ingratiating, we may mention the case of the typical neighborhood butcher during the meat-rationing period of World War II. Since the better cuts were scarce, the butcher tended to allocate the choice meat to those customers with whom he had developed friendly personal relations. The more unique he became as a source of choice meat, the more he undoubtedly found himself the target of a certain amount of ingratiation and flattery. Meat, which had formerly been allocated through the processes of impersonal economic exchange, was suddenly a customer benefit controlled by the butcher's approval and attraction.

Uniqueness is clearly of special importance in cases where ingratiation is used to evoke signs of worthiness. If signification is the goal mediated by ingratiation, then o's role as well as his level of information about p may be critical. P may not place much value on approval from just anybody, but he may be especially dependent on signs of approval from his minister, or his son, or his analyst, or his employer. Level of information or degree of acquaintance is similarly related to uniqueness. Approval by one who knows us only superficially will have less significance than approval by one who has seen us at our best and worst. (The reader will recall, however, that the level-of-information factor did not play a very crucial role in Gergen's 1962 experiment.)

Another consideration related to the uniqueness of the source of y is the possible production of y by p himself. Can p achieve y through his own direct efforts? If so, what is the cost of these efforts relative to the costs likely to be incurred by o in producing y? If y represents approval or manifestations of attraction, it is clear that p is in a poor position to provide these social benefits for himself. While it is certainly possible to strive for achievements worthy of self-approval or self-respect, approval and love and respect are ultimately anchored in the responses of others. With regard to other kinds of benefits, however, there may exist for p the option of securing y through his own efforts, versus inducing o to produce y for him. Here subjective cost estimates undoubtedly play a vital role. If p has a package to mail and the post office is further from his own commuting route than from that of his office-mate o, p may at least consider the possibility of getting the package mailed (y) by exerting social influence on o rather than taking the effort to go out of his own way. In such a case, of course, the differences in cost may be so apparent to o as well that a reasonable request from p is sure to succeed and no ingratiation would be required. Nevertheless, p might in subtle ways lay the groundwork for his request by avoiding disputes during the preceding hours, and by performing minor favors for o around the office. Thus we may suggest, as a corollary to the uniqueness proposition listed above, that the motive to be ingratiating to a particular o varies with the perceived difference between the costs likely to be incurred by p and o in producing the same y. The above example also suggests that when the cost differential becomes very obvious, providing the cost to o remains relatively low, ingratiation will be an unnecessary adjunct to a normatively binding, simple, request.

A third important factor involved in determining the magnitude of incentives to be ingratiating is o's *ability and disposition to produce negatively valued zs*. While o's capacity to help p may be salient, his capacity to hurt p may or may not be. If the symbol z stands for painful or unpleasant outcomes under o's control, then ingratiation may be adopted as a protective strategy (see chapter two). In this case y comes to stand for non-z outcomes rather than any specific benefit. As in our analysis of the case where y is of positive value to p, cost considerations are again important. While o may have the capacity to produce painful zs, it may be more or less costly for him to do so. Strictly speaking every o has the capacity to inflict harm on every p, but os are usually inhibited by cost factors involved in violating established social norms. Insofar as o's position is such that zs may be legitimately delivered—that is, delivered in a context of normative sanction—then p must calculate o's costs to produce z in other terms. It may require a certain amount of effort for o to produce z, as in the case where o considers paddling a fraternity pledge or decides whether or not to make sure a child stays in his room, and in general the *less* it costs o to produce z (behaviors unpleasant to p), the more p will be motivated to be ingratiating to o. The proposition refers to costs to o as perceived by p, and this may involve estimates of effort, time expenditure, or restriction of freedom (for example, if constant surveillance is necessary). Since y enters into a proposition which is the obverse of this, there is some point in talking about overall incentive value in terms of y minus z.

In this connection it is interesting to recall that Thibaut and Kelley (1959) formally define power as the range of outcomes through which one person can move another, and dependence as the range through which one can be moved. Since y minus z, in the current formulation, is equivalent to the range of p's outcomes controlled by o, we may summarize this section on incentive-based determinants by again noting that p will be motivated to ingratiate himself with o to the extent that p is dependent on o for providing (y) or removing (z) scarce resources.

2. SUBJECTIVE PROBABILITY OF SUCCESS

The incentive value of y minus z and the uniqueness of o as y's source are necessary but not sufficient determinants of ingratiation. Unless other conditions are favorable, even the most extreme dependence on approval responses from others will not initiate attraction-seeking tactics. One important class of further conditions is that set of variables associated with p's subjective probability that x will succeed in eliciting y and not z. The reference to z is important in this case, for if the possibilities are restricted to success or failure in eliciting y, there would be nothing beyond the immediate cost of producing x to prevent the occurrence of ingratiation. In other words, x would be very "low-risk" behavior—if it succeeds in elicting y, fine, if not, little has been lost. Considerations of z, painful or negative alternatives to y, remind us of the possibilities of boomerang. The transparent flatterer does not end up where he started when his blandishments fail; he loses ground and suffers from the attempt. The fact that most os have a fair capacity to produce such zs as hostility, mistrust, and avoidance, means that a variable amount of risk is involved in ingratiation attempts. The following discussion will keep this very much in mind.

Since we have treated the ingratiation episode as an errant member of the social exchange family, perhaps the first place to look for factors governing the subjective probability of success is in the *anatomy of the projected exchange*. From p's point of view (and we shall consistently adopt this point of view in the present section) how are the producible xs related to o's desires? Among the behavior alternatives available to p, are there any low cost xs which o will find valuable? If o is essentially satiated with approval, or if he has such strongly supported beliefs that agreement by one more p is incidental, or if he has such vast resources of goods and services that routine gifts would be superfluous, it is unlikely that the range of xs available to most ps would serve the strategic purpose of eliciting y. One has only to think in this connection of the problems involved in the exchange of gifts between heads of state. Obviously the secret is to provide a gift which is out of the stream of common economic exchange, one which is uniquely associated with the giver and not available for purchase or reproduction by the recipient. One might conclude that the more difficult it is for p to produce an x which o desires, the more p will be driven to make costly responses for o's consumption (the more costly, the less ingratiating), or to make no responses at all.

Under what conditions is o apt to be especially appreciative of, or vulnerable to xs that p can provide? In the case where x is expressed approval or admiration, the vanity or conceit of o seems especially relevant. Roughly nineteen hundred years ago, Plutarch noted the egotist's receptivity to flattery and we may now echo this with the statement that perceived conceit or vanity in o should raise for p the subjective probability that ingratiation will succeed. As we have previously noted, however, it is not simply a matter of how highly o thinks of himself, but also the perceived uncertainty of o's self-evaluation. Perhaps it is sufficient to build the subjective probability proposition around perceived vanity as long as we recognize that vanity and conceit are inevitably the covers for nagging self-doubts. In any event, just as the incentive value of attraction received by p is a function of p's needs for support and approval, so the value which o is judged to place on approval helps to determine the subjective probability of p's success in using tactics which imply attraction and support.

A further consideration which may enter p's calculation of probabilities is his judgment of o's responsiveness to the norms of distributive justice (Homans 1961). This norm may be loosely stated by modifying the biblical injunction to read, do unto others as they have done unto you. In chapter one we have suggested that one way of looking at ingratiation is to accuse p, the ingratiator, of capitalizing on o's adherence to the norm of distributive justice while he himself implicitly violates that norm. From the standpoint of predicting the success of an ingratiation attempt, it makes no difference whether o desired x *unless* the receipt of that x biases o positively toward p. There certainly exist people who consume favors and benefits with relish while impassively revealing no sense of obligation. Insofar as p perceives o to be such a person he is likely to decide that the delivery of x is an improbable condition for the receipt of y from o.

Another aspect of the anatomy of the exchange which is relevant to calculations of success probabilities is the saliency of y, the benefit desired, in o's response hierarchy. It might be said that the three ingredients for p's successful prediction of o's behavior are reliable information about the latter's capacity, his motivation, and the current state of his response repertory. O must not only be capable of producing y; he must be motivated to benefit p (that is, be biased in p's direction), and y must be a salient and appropriate response. To some extent, p can exert some influence on the saliency of o's responses by evoking relevant imagery or in other ways subtly arranging the proper situational props (see below). Such influence must be exerted with finesse and subtlety because of the importance of hiding the nature of the exchange involved. The goal of ingratiation is to effect a silent purchase of some desirable social commodity, and we would be very surprised to overhear such a statement as, "I have been agreeing with your comments lately because I would like you to ask me to your cocktail party tomorrow night," except, of course, in jest.

In addition to his ability to manipulate the saliency of y in o's repertory, p may have information which allows him to predict with some confidence that a particular y will follow any beneficial x. If o were known to be a compulsive philanthropist, for example, p could expect to be successful in soliciting money for his cause by tactics of ingratiation unaccompanied by specific pleas for an endowment. On the other hand, there are cases where o is favorably disposed toward p but remains unaware of the benefit which p really desires. The wife who abundantly demonstrates her love for her husband, but never mentions her respect for his professional skill, may be a case in point. Another example might be the son who wants more time with his father, but instead succeeds by his suppliant overtures only in securing increases in his allowance. Insofar as such difficulties are anticipated, and p cannot be confident of consummating a silent x-y exchange, he will be less likely to produce low cost x's or at least less likely to do so with much hope of success. Instead, p may be forced to produce x's whose cost is sufficiently high so that the exchange relationship no longer need be concealed. To return to the above example, the son can probably succeed in getting his father to spend more time with him by direct pleas, only to become beset with doubts about whether his father really wants to be with him or is merely responding dutifully to pressure. The more effortful alternative would be for the son to develop skills and interests similar to his father's so that y (time spent with son) becomes a naturally salient alternative in the father's repertory.

A second set of factors which influence p's subjective probability of success resides in the *nature of the p-o relationship*. In developing the argument about these factors we shall still be concerned with the anatomy of the exchange, but now with a special focus on the two participants and their complementary roles. We have already discussed some of the effects of power or status differences and we shall return for a closer look in chapter five, but these differences are again very relevant in the present context. Both power and status concepts suggests differential control over resources, but o's control over important ys has contradictory implications for p's probability of success in an ingratiation attempt. On the one hand, o's awareness of the value of his ys to the class of persons like p should operate to make the potential x-y exchange relationship more apparent to o. Thus the receipt by o of a low cost x might create resistance to influence to the extent that o realizes p's strong desire to receive y. By this reasoning, as o's relative power increases, p's subjective probability of success should decline. On the other hand, it is also probably true that as o's power increases (and therefore also his resources) it becomes easier and less costly for him to produce the valued ys for p's consumption. Since o's cost of producing y would begin to approach p's cost of producing x, the increasing visibility of the exchange should have less and less effect on the probability of p's success. Pointed examples of these contradictory effects are difficult to adduce, but it seems clear that a relatively powerful person who is intent on husbanding his resources will be more concerned about the deservingness of a recipient than a person with resources to squander will be. Perhaps evidence along these lines could be gathered from a survey of foundations and their response to applications varying in the proportion of substance to "grantsmanship." Or, to take a different example, the champion boxer may surround himself with a retinue of idle humorists, masseurs, and golf partners while the hungry challenger retains only the most productive and functional personnel. In a sense, the former can afford to support flatterers while the latter cannot.

The consideration of power differentials has additional implications for subjective probability of success. These stem from expanding our framework to include o's capacity to produce zs or unpleasant consequences for p. Power, it will be recalled, is the capacity to drive someone through a wide range of outcomes (Thibaut and Kelley, 1959) and is not determined solely by the magnitude of the best outcome in a person's control. From this definition it would follow that the more powerful o is relative to p, the more o has the capacity to hurt p. While p has more to gain by flattering a more powerful o, he also has more to lose— the possibility of boomerang becomes a more serious risk. P's subjective probability of success should be more a crucial determinant of his (explicit or implicit) decision to be ingratiating, the lower his power is relative to o's. High-power persons, however, can flatter and ingratiate others with relative impunity. It is our strong conviction that flattery from high- to low-status persons is indeed very prevalent. If one ponders the following two statements:

"You're an excellent man to have on the job, I'm glad you're with us."
"You're an excellent boss and employer, I'm glad to be working for you."

it seems clear that the frequency of some variant of the first would be much greater than of the second in most American organizations.

To pursue, for a moment, some additional reasons why this

might be so in the case of other-enhancement tactics, the upward communication of flattering compliments seems to violate the role prescriptions governing the behavior of persons low in power. It is presumptuous for an underling implicitly to claim the capacity to appraise a superior. As we have suggested in another context, a delicate additional problem is the dual meaning of a compliment: if an other-enhancing communication refers to some performance of the high-power person, it may implicitly convey to him the fact that the subordinate did not expect him to do so well. This would carry a particular sting coming from one who himself lacks experience, training, or requisite talent. Perhaps the best advice to give to an ingratiator bent on improving his power position would be to urge him to concentrate on self-presentation and conformity in order to make himself attractive. He should not worry about o's likelihood of producing y once he becomes attracted to p, for the risks of a boomerang are largely attendant on raising the salience of the x-y purchase relationship.

Probability of success is also affected by p's *control over situational resources*. To what extent can p manipulate or determine the time, place, and social context of his interaction with o? If p is restricted by the situation to one dimension of response (for example, agree-disagree) his opportunities for successful ingratiation will be less than if more dimensions of response are available. This may be stated more formally: the more variable the modes of x available, the greater the opportunities for successful ingratiation and the less the chance of a boomerang. This principle becomes an extremely important consideration in the design of experiments in this area. If two subjects are given high incentives to win attraction from each other in a free conversation, they will presumably explore mutual interests and common experiences and express their opinions in a highly differentiated and therefore highly credible way. If the same two subjects are restricted to the exchange of written opinion messages and one subject must report his opinion after being exposed to the other's opinion, the former should find it difficult to be ingratiating by agreeing closely with the latter in such a constraining situation. Results from the "Mike and Paul" experiment described earlier (Jones, Jones, and Gergen, 1963) show that subjects who observe one person continually agreeing with another end up with a negative evaluation of the conformist to the extent that he is presented as dependent on the other for approval. Two implications of this study for the present discussion would seem to be that subjective probability of success in an ingratiation attempt is reduced when (1) y is of clear and obvious importance to p and (2) when p's response options are sufficiently restricted so that there is little chance for communicative subtlety or complexity—that is, p is obliged to produce or not to produce a given x and is thereby deprived of many of the resources which lend credibility to an individual's statements.

In a recently completed experiment, Jones and Jones (1964) attempted to create a self-presentational dilemma from the fabric of these implications. That is, we designed a situation in which the subject (p) was clearly dependent on the target person (o), but his communication opportunities were so restricted that tactical maneuvers were difficult to execute. At least they were difficult to execute without being obvious to both p and o.

To summarize the experimental design, male subjects were instructed to exchange thirty opinion ballots with another person, the other person always expressing his opinions first. (The other person, in this case, was fictitious, his opinions actually being programmed by the experimenter.) The subjects had previously recorded their opinions in a "neutral" classroom setting, so it was possible to arrange the incoming opinion ratings to coincide with the subject's prior ratings on every item (*same* treatment) or to be systematically different from them (*discrepant* treatment). If the subject were to hold to, and reproduce, his originally stated opinions, he would present himself as behaviorally conforming in the *same* condition and as distinctly independent in the *discrepant* condition.

We reasoned that the subject in the *same* condition would find himself in a dilemma if his dependence on the target person were obvious—that is, if it were important to win the target person's approbation and the latter were clearly aware of his power in this respect. Under the circumstances the *same* subject could not remain true to his opinions without appearing to conform for ulterior effect. Since this would spoil his chances of creating a positive impression, or at least put his chances in jeopardy, the dependent *same* subject should attempt to avoid the appearance of over-conformity by modifying his initial opinions. If self-presentational accuracy rather than the management of a positive impression was his primary goal, however, the *same* subject should be more inclined to reproduce his prior opinion ratings with the (unintended) result of greater behavioral conformity.

Subjects in the *discrepant* treatment should be in an entirely different psychological position, and variation in the subject's dependence on the target person should have quite the opposite effect from that expected in the *same* treatments. We reasoned that the more important it was to create a positive impression, the more the discrepant subject would attempt to reduce the discrepancy between his opinions and the target person's—that is, to conform up to some moderate point. Combining the discrepancy variation, then, with some form of dependence variation, was expected to result in a statistical interaction effect: the attempt to create a favorable impression should lead to greater conformity in the discrepant treatment and less conformity in the same treatment than should an attempt to present a true, faithful, self-picture.

The dependence variable was manipulated by elaborate stage setting prior to the exchange of opinion ballots. In the *high-dependence* treatment, the experiment began with five subjects and the experimenter seated around a large conference desk. Prominently displayed on the desk were five place cards reading "Supervisor," "Production Manager," "Copy Writer" (two), and "Worker." On a nearby table were arrayed a stack of magazines, colored paper, scissors, glue bottle, and similar art supplies. After introducing himself, the experimenter informed the subjects he was studying productivity in groups with two different kinds of organizational structure. One arrangement had the person most attractive to the leader immediately under him in the chain of command, the other arrangement placed that person at the bottom of the chain of command. The experimenter then said the present group would be organized along the former lines to produce advertising copy—as he nodded to the supply of materials on the table. Next he enumerated the jobs in the work group and deliberately moved the place cards around the desk indicating where the jobholders would subsequently be located. The supervisor, he continued, would be selected at random by a roll of a die and the other positions would be determined by how attractive he judged each of the others to be on the basis of an exchange of opinions. The experimenter then stated that for the present group the person judged most attractive by the supervisor would be the production manager and the one judged least attractive would be the worker; the other two would be the copy writers. After relative attraction to the supervisor had been determined on the basis of an opinion exchange in another room, he continued, the group would return to the office, each would assume his assigned position around the desk, and together they would work for thirty minutes on advertising copy. The clear implication was that everyone would know how everyone else had been rated by the supervisor and it was expected that subjects would get emotionally involved in such a popularity contest.

Subjects in the *low-dependence* treatment were instructed in the same setting except that the place cards, magazines, and other art supplies had been removed. The experimenter explained that he was interested in what sorts of persons were "highly sensitive and accurate in their appraisals of other people." He indicated that earlier studies were open to question because they involved one person judging only one other and chance accuracy could never be ruled out. His innovation in this research was to have a judge who would make appraisals of four persons. In this way he could more carefully select accurate judges and compare their personalities with inaccurate judges. The test of a judge's accuracy, it was explained, was carefully controlled by only allowing him to have information about the others which he could gather from an opinion exchange. After stating that the judge for that session would be determined by a roll of a die, the experimenter emphasized that the other subjects had a delicate task too, because they would have to present themselves as honestly as possible in the opinion exchange if their judge was to have a fair chance of being accurate in his subsequent appraisals of them. Then the experimenter asked each subject to fill out a slip naming the two persons on campus who could give the best evaluations of him; these persons were to be contacted by the experimenter within the week. Ratings made by the two friends would be pooled with the subject's own rating of himself to determine the standard by which to compare the judge's accuracy. The experimenter concluded this part of the instructions by commenting that he hoped the judge from that group would prove to be highly accurate.

There is clear evidence from post-experimental questionnaire data that the two cross-cutting variations—opinion discrepancy and dependence—were effectively manipulated. Subjects in the *high-dependence* conditions expressed a greater concern with being liked ($p < .001$) and respected ($p < .001$) than subjects in the *low-dependence* conditions. Also, subjects in the *same* conditions perceived less opinion discrepancy than those in the *discrepant* conditions ($p < .001$), and also found the target person significantly more likable, sound, brilliant, and candid (in each case, $p < .001$).

Nevertheless, an important precondition for testing the major hypothesis did not obtain. In order for the *high-dependence same* manipulations to create the kind of "conformer's dilemma" we wished to study, it was important that the subject's opinions remained relatively stable over time. Circumstantial evidence from two control groups suggested that the amount of unsystematic opinion change in the experimental conditions was considerable. A first control group (C_1) was exposed to the high-dependence instructions in the experimental situation but in the opinion exchange these subjects always preceded rather than followed the prospective supervisor. A second control group (C_2) consisted of twenty randomly chosen students who twice filled out the opinion questionnaire—once near the beginning and once at the end of the semester. The average scale change per opinion item (direction disregarded) was 2.13 for C_1 and 2.09 for C_2. This means, in effect, that the opinions of subjects in the *same* conditions were not preempted by the bogus ratings coming from the target person, but were only fairly close to these bogus ratings on the average.

The unfortunate probable instability of opinion ratings was undoubtedly a factor in the results concerning accommodation to the target person's opinions. The main hypothesis of this investigation predicted an interaction between the two independent variables in affecting the final discrepancy between the target person's and the subject's opinions. A smaller discrepancy was predicted in the *low-dependence same* condition than in the *high-dependence same;* a larger discrepancy was predicted in the *low-dependence discrepant* than in the *high-dependence discrepant* condition. As Table 3 shows, the predicted interaction was indeed significant (along with both main effects), but the reversal of differences specified in the prediction did not occur. When there is a fairly sizable discrepancy between two persons' opinions and the importance of attraction is made salient, the individual who responds second attempts to reduce this discrepancy beyond that expected in a comparison condition where the initial discrepancy is as great but attraction is minimized. This part of the hypothesis was confirmed to a highly significant extent ($t = 5.03$, $p < .001$). When the initial discrepancy is minimal, however, the results do not show a reversal of this effect; instead, there is no reliable difference in resulting discrepancy as a function of the salience of attraction (that is, the dependence variable), and the mean difference is in the same direction as that in the discrepant conditions. As the significant main effect for dependence implies, pressures to be attractive produce change in the direction of conformity regardless of the degree of initial discrepancy, though the interaction tells us that this change is much greater when the discrepancy is substantial. The contributions of the discrepancy variable to the observed interaction probably reflect, in part, the fact that subjects in the *discrepant* conditions have more room for movement in the target person's direction than those in the *same* conditions.

The Jones and Jones study was mainly concerned with the potential dilemma facing subjects in the *high-dependence same* condition, with the remaining conditions serving as points of comparison. As originally planned, the dilemma was to emerge out of competing pressures to be true to one's own opinions while avoiding the appearance of slavish and manipulative conformity. In view of the instability of subjects' opinion ratings, and the resulting fact that their opinion during the experimental session

TABLE 3——Discrepancy from target and from before scores (comparison of experimental and control Ss)

EXPERIMENTAL Ss

		DISCREPANCY FROM TARGET*		DISCREPANCY FROM BEFORE SCORES†	
		high-dep.	low-dep.	high-dep.	low-dep.
SAME	X̄	1.47	1.67	1.47	1.67
	SD	.67	.37	.67	.37
	N	10	11	10	11
DISCREPANT	X̄	2.68	3.45	2.13	1.98
	SD	.46	.34	.38	.43
	N	15	13	15	13

CONTROL Ss

		LABORATORY (C_1)	CLASSROOM (C_2)
	X̄	2.15	2.09
	N	.56	.55
	SD	9	20

* These values represent the average difference per item between the subject's and the Target's opinion rating. Thus, the lower the discrepancy score, the greater the agreement with the Target. Comparisons: Same vs. Discrepant, $p < .001$; High vs. Low, $p < .01$; Interaction, $p < .05$.

† Since the Target's ratings are identical to the subject's ratings in the Same Condition, the means are the same in the first row of the table. In the third and fourth columns, the lower the score, the less the change (direction disregarded) from before to after rating. Comparisons between experimental and control Ss: Control $(C_1 + C_2)$ vs. High Same, $p < .02$; vs. Low Same, $p < .06$; vs. High Discrepant, n.s.; vs. Low Discrepant, n.s.

could not be accurately preempted by a repetition of their previously recorded ratings, there is serious question that such a dilemma was in fact created. The question remains serious in view of the failure of subjects in the *same* conditions to confirm the hypothesis on the discrepancy or conformity data. But there are interesting data from other sources which argue that a kind of dilemma *was* created in the *high-dependence same* subjects. For these subjects the problem was not, as initially proposed, one of remaining true to their own opinions while avoiding the appearance of conformity. Instead, the subjects faced a more benign dilemma: how to gain attraction and respect by conforming without appearing to conform and without having to acknowledge their conformity to themselves. What evidence is there that subjects in the *high-dependence same* condition faced such a dilemma and what may we say about their efforts to resolve it?

As described in greater detail in the original report of the experiment, the results for subjects in the *high-dependence same* condition differed in a number of respects from the results obtaining in other conditions. First of all, as may be seen in Table 3, *high-dependence same* subjects varied from each other in discrepancy score more than did subjects in the *low-dependence same* condition ($F = 3.2, p < .05$), suggesting greater conformity conflict in the crucial cell. Secondly, it turned out that those subjects in the *high-dependence same* condition who showed the greatest desire to be respected (on a post-experimental questionnaire) tended to avoid the extremes of great conformity and nonconformity in favor of moderate agreement. A third finding was that subjects in the *high-dependence same* condition expressed (on the average message to the target person) more confidence in their opinions than did subjects in all other treatments combined. Also, as Table 4 shows, only in the *high-dependence same* condition was there a high correlation between conformity and the amount of confidence expressed.

Thus it would appear that subjects in the *high-dependence same* condition showed evidence of conflict and attempted to find ways of convincing the other person of their sincere similarity of views. In part this was accomplished by the tendency of those who were most concerned with creating a positive impression to

TABLE 4——Relations between opinion conformity and confidence*

	HIGH-DEP.	LOW-DEP.
SAME	.671†	−.213
DISCREPANT	.076	−.149

* Note—See Table 3 for Cell Numbers.
† p <.05.

strike for an optimum level of conformity—to avoid the Scylla of overconformity and the Charybdis of errant disagreement. In part the conflict was resolved by making adroit use of the confidence ratings. A plausible interpretation of the correlation between confidence and conformity is that subjects who are concerned that they may have *agreed* too much, can attempt through high-confidence ratings to convince the target person of their autonomy in the agreement process. Those who are concerned that they may have *disagreed* too much can soften the impact of this disagreement by their lack of expressed self-confidence.

While these presumed tactics may be plausibly accounted for as part of a design to convince the target person of the subject's sincerity in expressing his opinions, there is additional evidence to show that the *high-dependence same* subject was also involved in convincing *himself* that his agreement with the target person was not manipulative in intent. Only in this condition was there a highly significant correlation between conformity and expressed liking for the target person (r = .774, p <.01). This can best be explained as an attempt on the part of the subject to justify to himself the validity of his expressed opinions. Since the measure of liking was taken from the post-experimental questionnaire, the favorable ratings could not have been part of any strategy to influence the target person. Instead, the correlation between conformity and liking seems a product of the subject's wish to emphasize (to himself and, perhaps, the experimenter) that agreement or disagreement was coincidental in the *high-dependence same* condition. By liking the target person the conformist in this condition may justify his conformity on grounds other than manipulative intent. To put the matter in a slightly different way: one likes another with whom one is in independent agreement. Therefore, the correlation reflects the subject's desire to believe the agreement is, in fact, accidental and his own opinions have been honestly recorded. The fact that the liking-conformity correlation occurs only in the *high-dependence same* condition (differing significantly, for example, from the low negative correlation in the *low-dependence same* condition) helps to rule out alternative interpretations. A more detailed discussion of these alternatives is presented in the full report.

The preferred interpretation, in the foregoing discussions, suggests that attraction may develop as a way of dealing with conflict or dissonance when conformity has occurred. The interpretation is quite reminiscent of that proposed by Gerard (1961a) to account for his results. The novel things about Gerard's experiment is that the subject was led to believe he had a strong tendency either to conform to group judgments or deviate from them. Much as in the present case, subjects who found themselves conforming to the group became attracted to the group as if to justify having conformed. This only happened when the subject believed himself to be capable in judging ability and thus could not easily justify his apparent conformity on the grounds that he was probably wrong and the group right. The high-ability conformer was in a state of high dissonance, according to Gerard's interpretation, and a convenient way to reduce this dissonance was to feel greater attraction for the group and thus have a reason for agreeing with the judgments of group members less able than he. (A fairly complete discussion of this experiment may be found in Brehm and Cohen, 1962, pp. 39–40.) The Gerard interpretation agrees with our suggestion that attraction to the group may increase as a way of reducing conflict or dissonance, though the precise function of the increase is somewhat different in the two experimental situations.

We have reviewed the Jones and Jones (1964) study at this point in the analysis of ingratiation phenomena because the results shed some light on the dilemma of attempting to create a positive impression with limited communication resources in a setting where the goal of impression management is salient to all concerned. Normally, the ingratiator may attempt to anticipate the opinions of a target person or find various ways to complicate and thus authenticate his posture of coincidental agreement. In the Jones and Jones experiment, however, the subject was forced to come to terms with the issue of conformity as a tactic of ingratiation because his communication possibilities were restricted to brief opinion ratings and accompanying statements of confidence. When the incoming opinions were quite discrepant with the subject's own, he responded to the dependence context by moving toward a position of compromise: while reducing the discrepancy between himself and the target person, sufficient discrepancy remained to make unnecessary any efforts to reassure the other or himself that he was not engaged in distorting his opinions for effect. When the incoming opinions tended to preempt his own, on the other hand, the high-dependence subject was faced with such a problem of dual reassurance. The results give a tentative picture of strategic behavior designed to certify the validity of opinions which happen to be in close agreement with those of the target person.

Returning once again to the question of subjective probability of success, another aspect of p's control over situational resources is his ability to maneuver o into settings where the saliency of the x-y purchase relationship will be low. In most cases of attempted acquisitive ingratiation, the primary goal of p is to bias o in his favor so that a particular y or class of ys will be a natural outcome of this or future interactions between p and o. We have been assuming that the greater the cost differential between x and y, the greater should be p's interest in obscuring the exchange component of their interaction. If p can create the circumstances where o can consume and enjoy x without being alerted to its relation to y, p can avoid a boomerang and has a better chance to exert a subtle influence on o's orientation to him. Thus, it is generally to the ingratiator's advantage to practice his art in contexts where his dependence on others is not salient. The prevalent belief that customers, buyers, or prospects, can be more successfully influenced over cocktails or in noncommercial social gatherings seems to bear ample testimony to the general argument. Indeed, it seems to be the case that the shoddier the product (x) that p has to offer, the more likely he is to seek out noncommercial contexts for the conduct of his business.

Finally, p's control over situational resources affects his subjective probability of success in still another way. By various means p may create the illusion that his x is more valuable, more costly to produce, than it would be judged to be objectively, or that y is *less* valuable in general or to p as an individual. Thibaut and Kelley (1959, pp. 119–122) discuss some of the various strategies by which one person may augment his power over another, and these involve attempts to manipulate o's perception of the relative value of x and y. Since we have restricted our attention to those exchanges in which the x-y exchange is mediated by attraction, a detailed discussion of manipulative power strategies would take us rather far afield. It is sufficient to note that p may be rewarded with o's attraction by in various ways convincing o that he is willing to take a loss in an exchange for the privilege of maintaining the relationship. As with regard to other antecedents of the ingratiation process, the more control p has over stage setting and situational management, the more confidence he should have in his ability to succeed in ingratiation and to avoid boomerang effects.

The attentive reader may have noted that the preceding account of ingratiation determinants seems to embrace a popular and familiar motivational model: goal-directed behavior is a joint function of the value of a goal and the subjective probability of success in achieving it. This model, or formula, goes back at least as far as 1940 with the paper by Escalona introducing the resultant valence notion, of which variants have appeared in the writings of Rotter (1954), Tolman (1955), and Atkinson (1957). It would appear, then, that ingratiation, or attraction-seeking behavior, is affected in its occurrence by the same formal factors which influence other kinds of performance—for example, those associated with task achievement and maze-running. Before we conclude this discussion of ingratiation determinants, however, there is an additional factor which must be considered, a factor which creates complications not ordinarily involved in other motivated behaviors: p's judgment of the legitimacy of the exchange involved in the ingratiation episode. The next section deals briefly with the issues involved in this third determinant of ingratiation.

3. PERCEIVED LEGITIMACY

We have defined ingratiation as an *illicit* attempt to win favor, and more loosely as an *illegitimate* member of the social exchange family. The decision to indulge in strategic conformity, other-enhancement, or artful self-presentation, is, then, a decision hedged by ethical constraints. We have argued in chapter three that such constraints do not necessarily prevent ingratiation but they often set the stage for self-deceptive cognitive work. At least when the ingratiation attempt is crowned with success, the undergraduate subject shows a readiness to treat his preceding actions as representative and accurate, thus avoiding the ethical implications of dissimulation. But the ethics of ingratiation are themselves complex in contemporary middle class society, suggesting that there are other avenues of self-justification available to the tactician. The individual may be aware that he is making a special effort to be liked, that he is telling white lies, and so on, but he may quite strenuously deny the immorality or illegitimacy of his behavior. Lack of awareness may thus be displaced from the falseness of the behavior to the immorality of being false. To the extent that the individual can convince himself that tactical maneuvering is morally justifiable and ethically legitimate, we should expect him to indulge more readily in such effect-oriented maneuvers. For this reason, perceived legitimacy is put forth as a third major determinant of ingratiation.

Many generations of scholars and commentators have grappled with the ethics of hypocrisy, dissimulation, and flattery. At the turn of the first century Plutarch wrote an essay, "How to Know a Flatterer from a Friend," which, in spite of its heavy moralistic tone, reveals convincing insight into the tactics of flattery. Through such insight Plutarch fulfills his purpose to instruct and to alert the reader to the various artful guises of the flatterer. In the process he presents the "parasitic" flatterer as a character type who is persistently devious and insinuating and constantly applying his arts toward immoral purposes. While the friend praises your virtues, for example, the flatterer "is ready to promote any base and unworthy action" (Plutarch, 1889 edition, p. 134). Thus the flatterer is not only "mutable and inconstant," he leads his victims into vice and temptation.

A brief survey of references to flattery and hypocrisy in various compendia of "familiar quotations" will reveal many comments which (along with Plutarch's) vehemently excoriate the flatterer. His evil is all the more pernicious and extreme because he is difficult to detect and deal with. Milton went so far as to call hypocrisy "the only evil that walks invisible, except to God alone" (*Paradise Lost*, Bk. iii, 1. 682). But most of the quotations on the subject listed in Stevenson (1934) and Bartlett (1882) mix righteous indictment of the flatterer with liberal criticism of those who succumb to the compliments of others:

> He that rewards flattery begs it.
> Thomas Fuller, *Gnomologia*, No. 2269

> He that loves to be flattered is worthy o' the flatterer.
> Shakespeare, *Timon of Athens*, Act I, sc. 1, 1. 232

> Every flatterer lives at the expense of the person who listens to him.
> La Fontaine, *Fables*, i, 2

Especially in Lord Chesterfield's "Letters" may one find flattery justified by the vanity, and therefore the gullibility, of the target person. Chesterfield, no doubt a decent man and a reader of Plutarch, walks a delicate tight-rope in advising his son:

Do not mistake me, and think that I mean to recommend to you abject and criminal flatteries: no; flatter nobody's vices or crimes: on the contrary, abhor and discourage them. But . . . if a man has a mind to be thought wiser, and a woman handsomer than they really are, their error is a comfortable one to themselves, and an innocent one with regard to other people; and I would rather make them my friends, by indulging them, than my enemies, by endeavoring (in that to no purpose) to undeceive them (1901, I, p. 28).

In a subsequent letter, Chesterfield reveals his own vulnerability in this respect and in refusing to complain, gives further justification for flattery and dissimulation as a natural response to man's nature:

Vanity . . . is, perhaps, the most universal principle of human actions; . . . I had that vanity, that weakness, if it be one, to a prodigious degree; and, what is more, I confess it without repentance: Nay, I am glad I had it; since, if I have had the good fortune to please in the world, it is to that powerful and active principle that I owe it. . . . If my insatiable thirst for popularity, applause, and admiration made me do some silly things on the one hand, it made me, on the other hand, do almost all the right things that I did. . . . With the men I was a proteus, and assumed every shape, in order to please them all: among the gay, I was the gayest; among the grave, the gravest; and I never omitted the least attention to good breeding, to the least offices of friendship, that could either please or attach them to me: and accordingly I was soon connected with all the men of any fashion or figure in town (1901, II, p. 139).

In contemporary American society the ethics of ingratiation are no less complicated and ambiguous. While it would be difficult to find a clear endorsement of insincere and manipulative social behavior in statements of the moral arbiters of our times, there is a vast grey area of moral ambiguity within which Dale Carnegie and others like him have been able to operate. The great success of *How to Win Friends and Influence People* (Carnegie, 1936) may itself say something about the modern American penchant for treating personality as a marketable commodity. In any event, the essence of Carnegie's confrontation of the ethics of deliberate impression management is that the right hand does not quite know what the left hand is doing. In a chapter entitled "How to Make People Like You Instantly," Carnegie expresses fury at the implication that he would compliment someone because he was trying to get something out of him ("Great God Almighty!!! If we are so contemptibly selfish that we can't radiate a little happiness and pass on a bit of honest appreciation without trying to screw something out of the other person in return—if our souls are no bigger than sour crab apples, we shall meet with the failure we so richly deserve" p. 131). And yet, the remainder of the chapter consists of a sequence of anecdotes in which the complimenter clearly gains material or social advantage from the target person, and this is the obvious message of the stories.

Carnegie takes an interesting tack in attempting to resolve his ambivalence about ingratiation and his conflict over being sincere and winning approval through compliments. He obliquely argues that a person will come to believe his insincere remarks and therefore they will cease being insincere. This is partly brought about by a kind of James-Lange theory of morality (if you act a certain way your feelings will come to reflect your actions) and partly by an appeal to see things from the other's (selfish) point of view. Along these same lines, an interesting and delightfully circular maxim appears in an earlier book by Webb and Morgan (1930) entitled *Strategy in Handling People,* "Personal charm arises chiefly from a feeling of deep and sincere interest in other people and a genuine liking for them. By acquiring the habit of success in dealing with people, you strengthen your interest in them and with it your power to charm them" (p. 158).

Dale Carnegie is both a reflection and a determinant of the ethical ambiguity which characterizes "applied human relations" in the masculine professional world. Both he and his many competitors tend to give concrete substance to the American business ethic and contribute a number of contradictory elements to it. Insofar as there are different standards or models of conduct to which one may repair, there is convenient room for variation in the perceived legitimacy of social accommodation. The sources of this variation lie in individual personality differences, in values common to a particular subculture or reference group, and in situational factors which contribute to definitions of appropriateness.

As for individual differences in personality, different emphases during socialization obviously can lead to important personality and value differences in adolescence and adulthood. A person may be taught in various ways to adopt a cynical view of human nature, allowing him to operate within a wider area of legitimacy than one with a less misanthropic view. Over a period of several years, Christie has been concerned with the measurement of individual differences in cynicism or misanthropy. We have already referred briefly to his Mach Scale, which was developed initially by paraphrasing statements from Machiavelli's *The Prince* and *Discourses*. Christie's original assumption was that individual differences in cynicism and attitudes toward manipulative influence could be measured by noting the frequency and degree of endorsement of these items. A number of versions of the Mach Scale have been developed, with studious attention being paid to the canons of proper questionnaire construction. It is by no means clear, as yet, what the Scale actually measures. However, Geis, Christie, and Nelson were able to show in a recent (unpublished) study that, relative to low-scorers on the scale, high-scorers applied themselves with greater zest and originality to the deception and manipulation of a peer in a pseudo-experimental setting. While this manipulation was legitimized by the experimenter, the results seem relevant to a search for individual differences in perceived legitimacy. It may be argued quite reasonably, at least, that low-scorers were less capable than high-scorers of dispelling their natural doubts about the legitimacy of the task, whereas a minimum justification was all that the high-scorers needed. As we find out more about the correlates of "Machiavellianism," we shall perhaps be better able to predict the differential responsiveness of subjects to instructions designed to elicit ingratiation.

Besides individual differences in the readiness to accept the legitimacy of tactical social behavior, there are undoubtedly subcultural differences in our society influencing the extent to which ingratiation is legitimized by the group. In the area of moral ambiguity which contains the practice of ingratiation, justifying the practice through social comparison with a relevant reference group would seem to be of critical importance. Depending on an individual's occupational role, his sex, and the social traditions of the region in which he lives, we would expect different normative base lines defining the extent to which candor should be bypassed in favor of supportive compliments and agreement. As we have indicated in chapter one, interpersonal behavior often involves the resolution of a tension which springs from the conflict between conveying accurate information and creating a social climate of warmth and positive feeing. A person's social origins and current status have much to do, presumably, with whether this conflict is resolved in the direction of informative candor or in the direction of kind and considerate accommodation. Just as we have been led to believe that the salutation, "darling," is repetitiously normative on the Hollywood production lot, other modes of address, other tactics of ingratiation are clearly more common in certain occupational subcultures than in others. The urbane courtesies of the organization man may contrast greatly with the jocular insults which are part of the norms of interaction on the assembly line. There is considerable informal evidence that courtesy, status deference, and warmth of greeting are generally more prevalent in the social behavior of Southerners than of, say, Bostonians or New Yorkers.

The matter of sex differences in the normative base line for ingratiation is an intriguing topic for speculation. With considerable trepidation, we would claim that the male in our society is more prone than the female to exploit the possibilities of ingratiation and to engage in its tactics for acquisitive and protective purposes. The female, on the other hand, may be more easily coaxed into compliments and agreements as part of a broader desire to make herself and others comfortable in the relationship. It has been our experience that female undergraduates can respond to instructions to create a favorable impression, but will resist if the legitimacy of doing so is not sanctioned by the experimenter. We shall present evidence in the next chapter which shows that male undergraduates tend to "rise to the bait" in a situation where it is fairly clear that their own acquisitive interests may be served by ingratiation. Perhaps males are more conditioned by the no-holds-barred business ethic in this respect. We have found that our female subjects are more reluctant to modify their self-presentations in the interests of personal gain, and that they express great discomfort when pressed to do so.

A counterpart of these alleged variations in the readiness of the two sexes to employ acquisitive ingratiation is a differential sensitivity to its practice. One might expect females to be more reluctant than males to adopt the hypothesis that someone else is being ingratiating, even though the context makes the hypothesis a very plausible one. If it is true that the average female in our society both gives and receives more supportive and less informative social behavior than the average male, this would seem to have rather definite implications for the development of her self-concept through the vicissitudes of social comparison. Is it possible that the female in our society is faced with special difficulties in establishing her identity, in knowing who she is and what she is capable of? Not only is she exposed to a more undifferentiated and saccharine information environment, but she has fewer nonsocial avenues than the male for assessing her relative standing on important self-dimensions. While the average male is constantly confronting tests which provide clear evaluative feedback (job assignments, raises and promotions, athletic competition) the majority of the tests which face the female result in feedback which is not only social but of the kind which is apt to be noncommittal and ambiguous. Whether these speculations can ever be confirmed by research, they seem to have sufficient plausibility to warrant further consideration and investigation.

Since an individual's decision to be ingratiating or not is conditioned by his personal history of exposure to relevant cultural norms, variations in the use of ingratiation tactics can only be studied against the backdrop of normative social behavior. It has been our strategy to attempt to separate the instrumental from the normative strains of flattery by the judicious use of control group comparisons and by concentrating on fairly homogeneous samples of undergraduate males or females. Even this kind of research strategy, however, still leaves open the possibility that there are cultural variations in the *proneness to adopt* ingratiation tactics as a way of securing approval or benefit. While we have been relatively successful in our attempts to induce effect-oriented social behavior in several equivalent samples of middle class students, there is considerable question whether the same independent variable manipulations would have the same effect with samples from different subcultures. Our belief is that similar effects could be produced with appropriate modifications tailored to relevant characteristics of other samples, but this is at present an optimistic and untested conviction. Attempts to transpose the logic of our inductions into new settings might be defeated either by the presence of unusually high normative base lines (in which case we would find a considerable amount of ingratiation in the control group) or by ethical resistance to the adoption of ingratiating tactics in the experimental (induced) group.

In addition to differences in individual values, which may or may not be easily derived from known subcultural norms, the perceived legitimacy of ingratiation is also affected by the immediate reference group context within which the individual actor, p, launches his interaction with o. Features of the contemporary setting define areas of behavioral legitimacy in combination with the kinds of personality and cultural factors we have just discussed. A moment's reflection suggests that there are organizational or social settings within which ingratiation is socially sanctioned or admired by relevant peers. To take one example, in a group setting where there are one or a few leaders and a number of involuntary followers, and where upward mobility is unlikely or remote in time (as in a basic-training company of draftees), these followers may give tacit or explicit support to ingratiating maneuvers initiated by one of their own members. This is especially true if the benefits sought (the ys) are group benefits, but even this is not an essential condition for group support. When the atmosphere is such that an inter-status relationship is largely antagonistic, the orientation of followers is often to beat the leader at the game of power application, to subvert, confuse, or thwart him in such subtle ways that reprisals cannot be legitimately applied. In such a situation, the follower who succeeds, by whatever nefarious strategies, in improving his own power position, is often applauded and admired by his peers. (A number of humorous motion pictures about life in the armed services have been based on this theme, a clear example being *Operation Mad Ball*. Sergeant Bilko, of the television series, provides another apt example.) Such a supportive reaction, we could imagine, is less likely to occur when (a) membership is voluntary, (b) possibilities of upward mobility and therefore inter-member competition are salient, and (c) followers accept ideologically the institutional arrangements which define the leader's superior power.

It is probably true, in general, that individuals can readily derive legitimizing support from fellow ingroup members for ingratiating themselves with members of an outgroup. Adroit use of ingratiation tactics has until recently been a major factor in the Southern Negro's *modus vivendi* with the Southern white. The Southern white has been a willing target for deferent and accommodating overtures from the Negro, partly because these overtures tended to confirm and reinforce his stereotyped view of racial caste differences. The Negro, for his part, has historically recognized that his interests are often better served by hypocrisy than candor when confronted with the superior power of the white person. Until the recent "Negro revolt," the Negro who ingratiated himself with a white person was at least tolerated by his fellow Negroes if not admired for his shrewdness in promoting his advantage by playing on (and incidentally reinforcing) the white Southerner's prejudices.

Judgments of legitimacy are also affected by certain coincidental aspects of the relationship between p and o and the attributes shared in common. Let us first consider the cluster of tactics which we have called other-enhancement. Other things being equal, p is more likely to compliment o the more o seems to deserve such compliments. This is a trite statement, but it has implications both for p's subjective probability of success in the ingratiation attempt and for his judgments concerning its legitimacy. If p can convince himself that o is really close to being a paragon, it is only mildly illegitimate to stretch the point by publicly assigning him paragon status. The same point may be made with regard to opinion conformity. It is morally easier to be ingratiating through agreement when another's opinions are close to your own, than when there are wide differences between respective beliefs. However, in keeping with the Jones and Jones (1964) study reported in the last chapter, it is quite possible that when actual (private) agreement is *very* close, p may express mild disagreement in order to increase his credibility and to avoid producing a boomerang effect.

In other words, ingratiation will be perceived as legitimate if (a) the target person is perceived as a natural enemy who does not deserve equitable treatment, and there is peer consensus to this effect; or if (b) the target person has positive attributes and judicious opinions in such abundance that an exaggeration of these virtues represents only the whitest of lies. These arguments seem to account for two extremes of a scale which leaves us with the implied proposition that ingratiation will be perceived as most *illegitimate* when o falls obviously short of paragon status, but when his intentions are nevertheless respected and he is viewed as worthy of honest and fair treatment.

At least two additional factors would seem to affect judgments of legitimacy, and one is the salience of the norms of distributive justice, candor, and observance of the rules which govern social competition. Except in the rather unique circumstances described above, in which p's reference group actually offers normative support for behaviors customarily viewed as ingratiating, we might expect the presence of bystanders to make salient the broader norms of interpersonal equity. For this reason, it seems appropriate to suggest that "flattery is a two-person game." The presence of a third, fourth, or nth person—evoking, so the argument runs, the norms of fair exchange—should sharpen the issue of legitimacy for p and inhibit his tendency to be ingratiating. This suggestion is obviously open to empirical study.

A final factor is the possibility that perceived legitimacy may develop out of a clear understanding of the plight of extreme dependence. While, in general, ingratiation directed toward improving one's position is frowned upon in our culture, it may be that we at least are more prone to tolerate tactical overtures when p has been dealt a severe blow by fate and when his needs for personal approval are understood to be high. From p's point of view, the fact that he finds himself in desperate need of y through no fault of his own may promote the convenient rationalization that ingratiating maneuvers are justified. The ingratiator may thus perceive that ingratiation is a legitimate (or at least an understandable) response to situational forces and it may be indulged in without implications for the self-image.

SUMMARY AND CONCLUSIONS

In this chapter we have attempted a systematic coverage of the motivational and cognitive determinants of ingratiation and flattery. While signifying and protective flattery have been alluded to on occasion, the emphasis has been on the more clearly acquisitive kinds of ingratiation. In order to facilitate and formalize communication, we have made liberal use of Heider's notational system and considered p, the potential ingratiator, and x, the potentially ingratiating response, in relation to o, the target person, and y, the particular benefit sought by p from o through the mediation of attraction. The determinants of ingratiation have been viewed as being fundamentally conditioned by p's perspective and therefore they are analyzable in terms of his unique life space. However, we have continually emphasized the manipulable or detectable environmental conditions which are most likely to affect p's cognitive and motivational state.

This systematic analysis of determinants has emphasized the dual role of evaluative and probabilistic considerations. That is, an individual will not enter into the low-cost area of ingratiation except to the extent that he desires a reciprocal benefit from the target person and he is confident that benefit, rather than harm, is likely to be forthcoming. The *incentive value* of the benefit, y, was seen to be a function of p's need or desire to receive y, the uniqueness of o as a source of y, and o's capacity and/or disposition to produce harmful zs rather than beneficial ys. The *subjective probability* of p's success in securing y was seen to be a function of o's need for x as perceived by p, the salience or position of y in o's response hierarchy, a complex of subtle factors involved in the exchange relations between p and o, and the extent to which p can exercise control over the setting in which x is to be produced.

We reported an experiment in which p had extremely low control over the setting and the importance of making a positive impression was clear to o as well as to p. The results showed how p's limited communication resources were used to conceal the ulterior significance of conformity from himself and from o.

A combination of high incentive and high probability of success may be a necessary, but not the only condition required for ingratiating behavior to take place. As the argument was extended in the preceding section, the analyst must also consider those factors which affect p's tendency to perceive the x-y exchange as illegitimate. Individual differences with respect to socially learned values obviously enter here, as do variations in perceived group support for besting an outsider. Perceived illegitimacy should also vary with the discrepancy between p's private and publicly expressed opinions and evaluations, and with such conditions of norm saliency as the presence of bystanders or observers. The fact that perceived legitimacy plays a role in the release or inhibition of ingratiating behavior brings us finally to a three-factor model of ingratiation.

Exactly how these three factors combine is, unfortunately, far from clear. It might be argued that the combination is multiplicative since if any factor is zero, ingratiation will presumably not occur. Intuitively, it may turn out that perceived legitimacy is more a dichotomous variable than either incentive value or subjective probability. Moral decisions tend to have an either-or quality about them. This would suggest that incentive value and subjective probability combine multiplicatively to produce a strong or weak tendency to ingratiate. Legitimacy then plays its role as a threshold factor, providing a go or stop signal for the behavior once the tendency to ingratiate reaches a certain strength. Thus a person may flatter or ingratiate even though he knows his behavior is illegitimate, once the importance and the likelihood of obtaining a benefit reach a certain combined value.

The fact should be emphasized that, while it is easier to talk about the determinants of ingratiation as if they fed into a conscious decision to impress and manipulate the target person, the decision is likely to be implicit and alternatives are readily blurred by p during or after the action in question. We might suggest, harking back to chapter three, that p normally arranges things so that the question of legitimacy is never raised in very sharp form, though the issue of legitimacy remains important as a determinant of the occurrence and form of ingratiation.

We are clearly not in a position to choose between competing formulations of the general model at the present time. Only the flimsiest empirical data are at hand, and even if one places undue weight on anecdotal material, it is by no means clear which formulation has the greatest plausibility or "antecedent probability." The present argument rests with the conclusion that incentive value, subjective probability, and perceived legitimacy seem to be conceptually distinct and empirically separable factors, each playing an important role as a determinant of ingratiation. The precise nature of this role is as yet unknown.

5 Power, Differences in Status, and Tactical Variations

In the preceding chapters, references to the role of power and status differences have appeared at almost every twist and turn of the analysis of ingratiation. The time has come to pull together some of these previous references and to clarify the implications of having and lacking power for the arousal and tactical form of ingratiating gestures. After this brief clarification it will be the main purpose of the chapter to present the results of two experiments designed to shed some light on the role of power differences, combined with other factors, as the determinants of effect-oriented behavior.

The study of ingratiation is closely connected with the study of power and power differentials. The very assumptions underlying our definition of ingratiation imply some kind of differential resources, for the motivational relevance of such behavior depends on the fact that the target person (o) has something the ingratiator (p) wants—whether it is a meaningful nod of approval, a higher salary, a promotion in rank, or some cooperative action. We have already accepted Thibaut and Kelley's (1959) general approach to the definition of power and dependence, and in so doing have endorsed the assumption that power differences

118

are *relative* differences in the ability of one person to move another through a wide range of outcomes. Inherent in this definition, then, are certain implications regarding the dependent position of the person low in power and his orientation to the resources which the high-power person commands. That these implications seem to us to be clear is indicated by the fact that in several of our experiments the condition in which ingratiation was expected has been labeled the *high-dependence* condition (Jones, Jones, and Gergen, 1963; Jones and Jones, 1964). The subjects in these conditions were placed by experimental induction into a position of needing a positive appraisal from a target person. Since the target person had the potential to give or withhold approval, we might say that he had power over the subject in that respect.

The experiments to be described in the present chapter are more concerned with power relations within a fairly well-defined organizational structure. In the first experiment a cluster of variables defining potential power within a Naval ROTC unit were reinforced by instructions intended to create clear differences in overall power position. Since power variations in this experiment were in fact only implied by emphasizing attributes correlated with command over resources in a typical military unit, the report of the study speaks of status differences rather than differences in power. The second experiment also trades on certain attitudes developed in organizational settings where there is a clear division of superordinates and subordinates, though the experiment is actually presented as a game circumscribed by the immediate experimental setting. These two studies were designed in a partly deductive and partly inductive attempt to move beyond the self-evident notion that one is more motivated to be ingratiating when he lacks resources than when he commands them. The first study (Jones, Gergen, and Jones, 1963) explored the differences in attraction-seeking tactics as a function of position in a status hierarchy. The second study (Jones, Gergen, Gumpert, and Thibaut, in press) attempted to specify some of the major variables conditioning a subordinate's decision to ingratiate himself with a superordinate.

AN EXPERIMENTAL STUDY OF TACTICAL VARIATIONS AS A FUNCTION OF POSITION IN A STATUS HIERARCHY

This study was prompted by certain reflections on the social behavior of leaders and followers in task-oriented groups. Our previous comments on the links between dependence and ingratiation would suggest a certain impetus for follower-to-leader attraction-seeking, but does it make sense to suggest that the *less* dependent member of a dyad would ever seek to ingratiate himself with the more dependent member? Unless one fantasies about organizational settings which are totally autocratic in structure, an interesting feature of most status hierarchies is that the subordinate and the superordinate are both in various ways dependent on each other. The low-status person is dependent on his superordinates for task definition, performance evaluation, opportunities for advancement, letters of recommendation, and so on. The high-status person is dependent on his subordinates for their efficient labor, for their loyalty to the organization, and in more complicated ways for signs of his own success as a leader. In addition, in more complex organizations the leader may be more favorably evaluated by *his* superiors if he can inspire the loyalty and spontaneous affection of his crew. Finally, both the leader and the follower undoubtedly import a general need to be liked into the organizational situation, and therefore winning the affection of another person may represent a gratifying conquest for both subordinate and superior.

If we acknowledge that both superiors and subordinates can, on occasion at least, be motivated to make an especially attractive impression on each other, the questions become *how* they go about this, and whether the tactics employed vary as a function of position. Much has already been said concerning the psychological position of the person who obviously needs a commodity, access to which is controlled by another. By extending these earlier observations to cover the case of the low-status person, we may get some insights into the problems facing an ingratiating subordinate. The low-status subordinate (p) is in the position where the incentive value of approval and other rewards (y) is relatively high, but the subjective probability of an ingratiating gesture (x) leading to y is relatively low. In other words, the low-status person is highly motivated to be liked by the high-status leader, but his position is so obvious in this respect that some of the more direct and obvious tactics of ingratiation may seem risky and inopportune. In addition, the low-status person must avoid any behavior which implies that he is competing with, or usurping the position of, the high-status person. In a recent book, Blau (1964) presents a penetrating analysis of the emergence and maintenance of status differences in small groups. He suggests that the paradox of attraction-seeking (or in his terms social integration) is that the impressive qualities which make a person a particularly valuable and attractive associate also constitute a status threat to the others. While an appointed or institutionalized leader has a certain amount of invulnerability to such threats, he nevertheless retains some sensitivity to blatant competitive moves from below.

From such reasoning we may extract the general hypothesis that low-status persons, vis-à-vis those higher in status, will confine their ingratiating maneuvers to more oblique and subtle tactics and will operate most boldly and brashly in those areas in which their communications are less likely to reveal ulterior, acquisitive motivation. If we now consider the three tactics presented in chapter two—other-enhancement, conformity, and self-presentation—there are reasons why conformity might seem to be the most appropriate for the typical subordinate. Conformity to the opinions of the leader is effective because it is difficult to discriminate between conformity and genuine attitude similarity; opinion agreement bolsters the validity of the leader's views without raising obvious questions about devious intentions. The high-status recipient of agreement is not likely to suspect its tactical origin because, from his perspective, it is gratifying but hardly surprising when people believe what is "correct." (As argued in chapter two, however, the low-status person must not appear to be *changing*, without resistance or intervening thought, from initial disagreement to agreement with the high-status superordinate.)

The other-enhancement tactic seems less appropriate for

the low-status person because his evaluations are based on standards of unknown validity (he may be perceived as comparing the leader's attributes to those of low-status people like himself), and because the use of direct compliments is such an obvious tactic and one which can be exercised at low emotional or intellectual cost. Nor are tactics involving modesty of self-presentation likely to play an important role for the low-status person. As Blau (1960, p. 550) argues, if a person is not at all impressive to begin with, self-deprecation can only embarrass others and tends to make the unattractive person even less attractive. On the other hand, the risks of public self-aggrandizement have already been touched on. Not only is there a general problem of appearing boastful and conceited; there is the more specific problem of appearing to usurp those attributes correlated with status and impressiveness.

The psychological position of the high-status person is quite different. While for reasons cited above the leader may be motivated to seek the follower's approval for the way in which he is handling his role, and beyond this the follower's affection for him as a person, the incentive value of these ys is typically lower than in the case of the low-status person. While it is comforting to be judged an attractive person as well as a skillful leader, there is apt to be less urgency attached to the attainment of this goal. On the other hand, the risks entailed in ingratiation and the ethical constraints involved are both likely to be lower in the high-status case. As compared with the low-status ingratiator, the high-status tactician will have a higher subjective probability of success, and he will tend to perceive the exchange of his ingratiating overtures (x) for approval and loyalty (y) to be a legitimate part of his role. One reason why his subjective probability of success is apt to be relatively high may be the fact that persons low in status are likely to underestimate their counter-power, or the importance attached by their superordinates to the loyalty and affection of subordinates. And even if the low-status follower perceives the leader to be going out of his way to curry favor, he may place a benign cast on his motives for doing so and see him as acting for the good of the organization (to improve morale) rather than for obvious personal gain.

The high-status person's position enables him, then, to reduce the normal risks associated with ingratiating overtures even though signs of approval may be of less over-riding importance to the leader than they are to the follower. Nevertheless, the leader does confront a particular problem or dilemma in his attempt to enlist the liking and spontaneous loyalty of his subordinates. He must win the subordinate's support, which involves elements of affectional attraction, without undermining his own respectability and power. In surveying the three available tactics of ingratiation, the tactic of conformity seems most vulnerable to these considerations. At some point in his interactions with the subordinate, the high-status leader must demonstrate his capacity to form independent judgments in areas where his experience and his role render him likely to be more competent than the subordinate. While the leader may seek out opinion issues on which he can safely agree with his subordinates, he has much to lose if his conformity is indiscriminate. Also, the leader who adopts the tactic of conformity soon finds that he cannot agree with all of his subordinates, unless they agree among themselves.

In many leadership contexts, however, the more direct tactic of other-enhancement may commend itself to the high-status person. To evaluate someone positively to his face implies that you are in a position to pass judgment—a consideration which is in line with the status differential characterizing the relationship. One risk involved, however, is that the low-status person may exploit the superordinate's compliments to press for favored treatment, higher salary, or the like. The leader who passes out compliments in private dyadic pep talks also runs the risk of alienating followers in the event that the subordinates begin to compare notes and discover either that each has been ritually praised in the same manner, or that there have been obvious discrepancies between face-to-face and behind-the-back appraisals.

The leader is likely to be especially concerned with effective self-presentation in his communications to the subordinate. Blau (1960), for example, feels that the high-status person faces the problem of impressing others without causing them to lose their affection for him (though he is somewhat uncertain about the importance of this affection as long as the leader's talents are highly needed). The more impressive a person becomes, the more unapproachable he becomes (p. 547) and the more difficult it is to initiate social interchanges with him. The tendency for respect and liking to be inversely correlated—insofar as respect implies high impressiveness—is sometimes handled by the sharing of leadership roles between a task leader and a social-emotional leader (cf. Bales, 1958). When this is not possible, however, the high-status person must find ways to demonstrate his approachability without at the same time destroying his impressiveness or his follower's respect for him. As Blau implies, he may do this (a) by emphasizing such shared characteristics as ethnic background, interest in the sports news; and/or (b) by presenting himself in a self-deprecating manner. But the self-deprecation cannot be indiscriminate. The high-status person must not deprecate himself on those characteristics central to his status. This would serve only to undermine the basis of the subordinate's respect for him. He must demonstrate his approachability by acknowledging actual or alleged defects on nonsalient, unimportant attributes. For the high-status person, then, an appropriate tactic of ingratiation (or approachability demonstration) involves a pattern of self-presentation wherein important positive traits are readily acknowledged along with an emphasis on weaknesses in nonessential areas.

In order to investigate the validity of this tentative and informal reasoning, an experimental situation was devised so that at various points in the procedure high- and low-status pair members communicated with each other about opinion issues, about the characteristics of the other person, and about the self. The conditions of communication were carefully controlled. In order to arouse motives to ingratiate, subjects during the first year of the study were instructed concerning the vital importance of mutual compatibility. In an attempt to provide a control comparison with subjects communicating under low-ingratiation incentives, different subjects during the second year were urged to be themselves and to avoid misleading the other person about their true nature. Given such settings, it was possible to investigate whether:

1. Low-status subjects show a greater tendency to conform

on opinion issues than do high-status subjects. This tendency toward differential conformity should be especially pronounced when instructions have emphasized compatibility and when the issues being discussed are relevant to the basis of the status hierarchy.

2. In presenting their self-ratings to the other person, high-status subjects under instructions emphasizing compatibility show a greater tendency to deprecate themselves on nonimportant versus important attributes than low-status subjects. Without the compatibility instructions the difference between high- and low-status subjects should be smaller.

3. Low-status subjects show a greater tendency to refrain from overtly flattering high-status subjects than do high-status subjects from flattering low-status ones. This should especially be the case given high compatibility incentives.

In order to fulfill the experimental purpose, we had to find an existing organization in which status differences could be easily located and reinforced by experimental procedures. Members of high- and low-status positions in the hierarchy then had to be brought into a communication situation in which there could be an exchange of opinions on a variety of issues, each person would have a chance to describe himself to the other on dimensions lending themselves readily to subsequent measurement, and each would transmit to the other his evaluations of the other on these same dimensions. Furthermore, it was important that each subject received exactly the same information from the other so that variations in responses would be a function of the experimental conditions and not a second order function of variations in information received. Finally, and most important, some way had to be found to vary the importance of making an attractive impression and to accomplish this in a manner which would apply pressures of similar magnitude to both high- and low-status communicators. The following account of procedures designed to achieve these objectives is a condensation of the more detailed description in the original report. The results will also be selectively presented here, though we shall attempt to be faithful to the entire pattern of findings and shall present the major results in fair detail.

METHOD

The subjects in the experiment by Jones, Gergen, and Jones (1963) were seventy-nine undergraduate male volunteers from the Naval ROTC unit at Duke University. Subjects participated in the experiment in groups of four. Each group was composed of two freshmen and two upperclassmen (either juniors or seniors), hereafter designated as LS and HS subjects. Because the population sampled was quite small, it was necessary to run the experiment over a two-year period. During the first year (*ingratiation condition*) the experimenter introduced the study as one concerned with testing naval leadership potential. More specifically, subjects were told that previous attempts to develop such tests in real-life settings had foundered because commanders and subordinates had not always been initially compatible. The purpose of this study was allegedly to find out if "compatible groups provide a better setting in which to test leadership potential than do incompatible groups." In order to answer this question, subjects were told that leadership tests would be given during drill periods later in the year:

In these tests, we are going to observe different two-person groups. Some of these will be compatible and some will be incompatible. Each test will involve one commander (in other words, an upperclassman) and one subordinate (a freshman). Today we are going to make up two commander-subordinate pairs simply by putting one upperclassman and one freshman together, and we are trying to make a determination of the degree to which each pair is compatible. After forming the pairs, in other words, we want to find out whether the commander ends up thinking highly of the subordinate and whether the subordinate ends up liking and respecting the commander (Jones, Gergen, and Jones, 1963, p. 5).

In order supposedly to control factors associated with physical appearance, it was explained that each subject would communicate from a private booth to the other member of his pair without knowing the exact identity of this member.

In order to increase the incentive to be compatible each of the four subjects was asked to identify himself by name before being ushered to the booth, and each was then asked to write down the name of the person in the other status level he would most like to have as his partner in the experiment. Once inside the booths, each subject was told that he would be communicating with a person who had expressed a preference for working with him. He was then told:

It looks like there is a good chance that you will end up being a compatible pair if it turns out that you like him, and he does not change his mind about you. For this reason I hope that you will make a special effort to gain his liking and respect, always remembering your position as commander [subordinate] (p. 5).

Each of the second-year sessions (*control condition*) was presented to the subjects as an attempt to study how leaders and followers can get to know each other. The emphasis was on the importance of obtaining valid information in forming an impression. The orienting instructions concluded with the following reminders:

We are interested in studying how well each of you can do at learning the kind of person the other is when there are differences in status. Therefore, it is especially important that each of you respond naturally and thoughtfully when it is your turn, and that you do not try to mislead the other person or to confuse him. He is going to want your frank and honest opinions in order to form an accurate impression of you. Keep in mind, then, the importance of being yourself. . . . We are not especially concerned with whether you end up liking each other or not. This is not the point of the experiment. We are interested only in how well you can do in reaching a clear impression of the other person (p. 5).

The anonymity of each subject was assured.

Except for these orienting instructions, subjects in the control condition were exposed to the same subsequent procedures as subjects in the ingratiation condition. These procedures will now be described.

Procedures for exchanging information. Once each subject was seated in his own private booth, it was possible to intercept all outgoing communications and to provide each subject with standard messages. These were allegedly from the unknown different-status partner. Thus at no time did subjects actually communicate with each other, and HS and LS subjects were exposed to identical information from outside.

The first task for each subject (the *opinion exchange*) was to transmit his ratings on twenty-four assorted opinion items to his partner. Each item appeared on a different ballot or message form. Half of the opinion messages were initiated by the subject, sent to his "partner" and then returned to the subject—appearing with a bogus statement of the partner's opinion alongside his own. The other half of the messages, those with which we will be primarily concerned, were presumably initiated by the partner, received by the subject (who then indicated his own opinion beneath that of his partner), and then returned presumably to that partner. Nine of the twelve opinions received were highly discrepant from norms which were established earlier on an equivalent population. Our measure of conformity was the degree of discrepancy between the subject's own recorded opinion and the rather idiosyncratic opinions received. It should be noted that the validity of such a measure depends on the assumption that a given subject would have scored at or near his class norm in the absence of experimental influence pressures.

A very important feature of the opinion messages—one designed to increase the theoretical precision of the analysis—was that the items fell into three classes of content, varying in their relevance to the basis of the hierarchy. Three of the critical items involved opinions about highly relevant Navy matters, such as whether Annapolis graduates should be given positions of authority over ROTC graduates of comparable seniority; three items concerned issues of intermediate relevance to the hierarchy by dealing with opinions about college courses, fraternities, and so on; a final set of three items involved general issues quite removed from the specific basis for the status differential and were miscellaneous in content.

After the opinion exchange, the subject's next task involved an *exchange of self-presentation* ratings with his partner. To this end, each subject was asked to fill out a fairly elaborate rating scale appraising his own characteristics. He was also instructed to check a box in the margin beside any dimensions which he felt denoted particularly important personal characteristics. He was clearly told that his ratings were to be transmitted to the partner, though actually again a standard form was delivered so that each subject received an identical set of self-ratings presumably coming from the other.

The subject was finally instructed to indicate on the same rating scale his own *appraisal of the other* person, again under the illusion that this would be transmitted back to that person. The way in which the subjects used the third scale to evaluate the partner for transmission to him constituted the measure of other-enhancement. While subjects were making these ratings, bogus ratings of the subjects were being recorded on the subject's self- and ideal-rating sheets. These ratings were also the same for all subjects and were uniformly toward the positive extreme of the scale. These rating forms, earlier initiated by the subjects and now containing bogus ratings of them presumably made by the partner, were then returned to the subjects for examination. It should be mentioned that twelve HS and twelve LS subjects in the control condition were instructed that these ratings of the partner would *not* be transmitted to him. All remaining subjects filled out their evaluations of the partner after clearly stated instructions that these evaluations would be transmitted to him. This return versus no-return variation was included to check on the effects attributable to the knowledge that the other was to see how he was rated by the subject.

Finally each subject was asked to make a series of *private evaluations* of his partner. These were not to be exchanged but allegedly, in the ingratiation condition, were to be used to make the preannounced crucial judgments as to the compatibility of the pair. The private ratings did not have the same significance for subjects in the control condition. Included on the private rating form were a number of questions regarding the subject's perception of the partner's sincerity, and questions dealing with the efficacy of the experimental manipulations.

RESULTS

Opinion Conformity. An Index of conformity was constructed by recording for each of the twelve critical items, the degree of discrepancy between the subject's rating and the modal response of ROTC classmates (not participating in the experiment) to the same item. Discrepancy was always measured, of course, in the direction of the bogus rating received on a given item. Figure 2 graphically illustrates the conformity data. It is evident from Table 5 that each of the experimental variables contributed a significant effect. The LS subjects conformed more than the HS subjects; on the average, subjects conformed

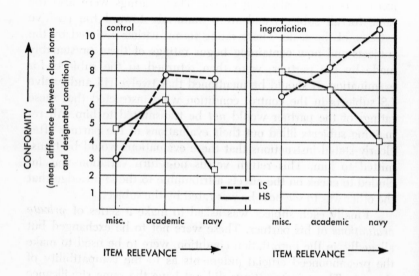

FIGURE 2——Conformity as a function of issue relevance

more in the ingratiation condition than in the control condition; and, there was a general tendency to conform less on academic items than on either Navy or miscellaneous items. (It might also be noted in passing that there was a significant amount of social influence in eleven out of twelve comparisons between subject means and class norms. Only in the HS control condition

TABLE 5——Opinion conformity: summary of analysis of variance*

Source	df	MS	F
BETWEEN SUBJECTS	75		
ingratiation versus control (B)	1	186.12	5.38†
HS versus LS (C)	1	208.44	6.02†
B × C	1		.07
error (b)	72	34.62	
WITHIN SUBJECTS	152		
relevance (A)	2	73.44	5.88†
A × B	2	32.64	2.61
A × C	2	154.21	12.35‡
A × B × C	2	2.76	
error (w)	144	12.49	

* For this analysis, cell frequencies were equalized by randomly discarding subjects in the larger cells.

† p < .05.

‡ p < .01.

with the Navy items did the mean fail to differ significantly from the class norm.)

Interpretation of the main effects, and especially the effect of relevance, must await consideration of the highly significant interaction between status and relevance. In both the ingratiation and control conditions, LS subjects conformed more than HS subjects only on the items most relevant to the basis for the hierarchy. This tendency was especially clear (see Figure 2) in the ingratiation condition, where increasing relevance led to more conformity in LS subjects and less conformity in HS subjects. However, when separate analyses are performed the interaction between status and relevance is highly significant in both the ingratiation condition ($F = 6.87, p < .01$) and the control condition ($F = 5.39, p < .01$).

It would appear that a rather general tendency exists for the high- and low-status persons to show differential conformity to the extent that the issues involved are relevant to the basis of the hierarchy, and that this tendency is not markedly affected by variations in the importance of being liked. What *is* affected by the arousal of ingratiation motives, however, is the overall level of conformity behavior manifested. Both HS and LS subjects conform more under pressures to be ingratiating than when specifically cautioned to express their true views. This is not particularly surprising, perhaps, but it does help to validate the manipulations conveyed by the two sets of orienting instructions.

Self-presentation.   In describing, above, the psychological position of the leader, we presented a hypothesis suggested by Blau (1960) referring to the potential conflict between impressiveness and approachability. The present version of the Blau hypothesis holds, in effect, that the high-status person is more likely than the low-status person to emphasize his positive attributes in important areas and to deprecate himself with respect to less important traits. By implication from Blau's argument that this is the leader's way of demonstrating approachability while maintaining the follower's respect, this tendency should be especially pronounced in the ingratiation condition.

In the present experiment, the importance of an attribute was determined by each subject for himself. The average subject checked about one out of every three items as important, and there were only negligible differences between the mean number of items checked in each cell of the design. In analyzing the data to test the Blau hypothesis, two separate scores were derived for each subject: the average rating assigned to important and unimportant items respectively. Since each of the twenty-four scale items consisted of one highly favorable and one unfavorable antonym, this average rating was assumed to reflect the favorability of self-description at one of two levels of judged im-

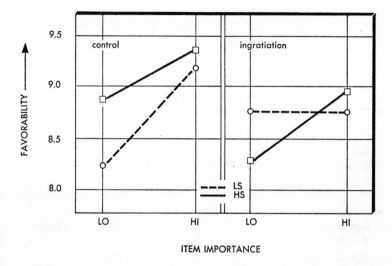

FIGURE 3——Favorability of self-presentation on items varying in importance

portance. The means for each cell are portrayed in Figure 3, and the results of the variance analysis are shown in Table 6.

Within the ingratiation condition, the Blau hypothesis seems to be confirmed. There is no main effect of status or importance, but the predicted interaction is significant ($F = 4.19, p < .05$). Thus HS subjects in the ingratiation condition did describe themselves more favorably on important than on unimportant traits, and there was no such tendency for LS subjects.

When the results for the control condition are also considered, however, and when the full analysis is examined (Table 6), matters become more complicated. Here we see that there is an overall main effect of the within-subjects' variable, importance. The attributes which are designated as important by the subject tend to receive more favorable ratings. As Figure 3 shows, the one exception to this general effect occurs in the LS ingratiation cell. This exception is marked enough to produce a sig-

TABLE 6—— Self-presentation: summary of analysis of variance

Source	df	MS	F
BETWEEN SUBJECTS	67		
ingratiation versus control (B)	1	2.73	
HS versus LS (C)	1	.40	
B × C	1	2.12	
error (b)	64	2.44	
WITHIN SUBJECTS	68		
importance (A)	1	9.23	17.03*
A × B	1	1.44	
A × C	1	.06	
A × B × C	1	3.60	6.64†
error (w)	64	.54	

* $p < .001$.
† $p < .05$.

nificant second-order interaction between status, condition, and importance. As a function of increasing the pressure to be liked, HS subjects became generally more modest in presenting themselves. In keeping with the Blau hypothesis, this tendency was somewhat greater for the unimportant than for the important items. In contrast, when ingratiation pressures were applied to LS subjects, they became slightly more modest about the important attributes and considerably more favorable in presenting their unimportant traits. As a result, when one considers only the approximately sixteen items not checked as important, the HS subjects became significantly more modest when trying harder to be liked ($p < .02$) while the LS subjects became less so ($p < .06$).

Other-enhancement. It will be recalled that each subject rated his partner on the same twenty-four antonyms that he had rated himself on, and these ratings were presumably transmitted to the partner. As with the self-presentation data, the "other ratings" could be converted into favorability scores by the simple method of summing the raw scores for each evaluative antonym. The resulting picture is not very illuminating, but the pattern of means certainly gives no support to the hypothesis that HS ingratiators would be more flattering in their ratings than LS ingratiators, both relative to ratings of HS and LS control subjects. In point of fact, LS subjects in the ingratiation condition were significantly more positive in their ratings than LS subjects in the control condition. Other ratings of the HS subjects, on the other hand, were not affected by the variation of ingratiation-control instructions. If anything, then, the hypothesis that other-enhancement would be the preferred strategy of the HS subjects, and the nonpreferred strategy of the LS subjects, is directly controverted by the data.

Apparently our reasoning concerning the obviousness and riskiness of flattery from LS to HS persons was not shared by the college freshmen in the experimental sample. They clearly responded to the ingratiation instructions by transmitting more positive evaluations to their HS partners. However, there is at least some evidence that their choice of this strategy was a reckless one under the circumstances. It will be recalled that all subjects in the ingratiation condition and approximately half of the subjects in the control condition received identical sets of highly positive other-ratings from their partners. This confirmed the understanding that each subject's other-ratings would be transmitted to the target person in the ingratiation and control-return conditions. Subjects in the control no-return condition did not receive the other's ratings of themselves, in line with the experimenter's assurances. Later, each subject responded to three scale items, imbedded in the "private" post-experimental questionnaire, which were designed to form a rough measure of perceived flattery. The results of a comparison of perceived flattery scores across the various experimental conditions are presented in Table 7. It is apparent that in the ingratiation condition, HS subjects attributed more flattering intentions to LS subjects than vice versa (p < .01). This difference disappeared completely in the control conditions. It is also clear that whether or not the subject received a final set of positive ratings (return versus no-return) made little or no difference in these differential attributions of flattery. Either the ingratiation instructions alone, or the combination of these instructions with the high degree of rigged conformity-to-the-subject during the first message exchange, were sufficient to alert the HS subject to the likelihood that deceit and flattery might well be involved in the communications received. It is interesting to note that the LS subjects became *less* suspicious in the ingratiation condition, suggesting, perhaps, an eagerness to take the compliments and agreements received at face value. While a number of additional

TABLE 7——Perception of flattery (mean* postexperimental ratings in each condition and differences between them)

CONDITION†	GROUP						
	HS			LS			
	M	SD	N	M	SD	N	p DIFF.
INGRATIATION	13.05	4.14	19	9.62	3.16	21	.01
CONTROL							
TOTAL	11.68	4.46	19	11.85	3.41	20	ns
RETURN	11.71	4.26	8	12.25	4.58	8	ns

* These means are based on the following items: completely sincere—on the phony side, trustworthy—unreliable, brutally frank—flatterer. The higher the mean score, the greater the perceived flattery.

† Comparisons across conditions—Ingratiation (HS-LS) versus control (HS-LS): $t_{74}(13.05 - 9.62) - (11.68 - 11.85) = 2.101$, p <.05. Ingratiation (HS-LS) versus control-return (HS-LS): $t_{51}(13.05 - 9.62) - (11.71 - 12.25) = 1.690$, p <.10.

treatments would need to be included before an unequivocal interpretation could hopefully be found, the results seem to illustrate the dangers of attempts at ingratiation when the actor is in a position of low-power, or low-status, and when instructions have emphasized each person's stake in being attractive to the other. On the other hand, compliments and conformity moving downward in a hierarchy tend not to raise questions about sincerity and frankness. If we combine the fact that LS subjects conformed and flattered freely in the ingratiation condition, with the fact that their motives were suspected by the HS subjects, we are led to the notion (which seems worth pursuing) that effect-oriented subordinates cannot resist expressing complimentary evaluations to a superordinate even though this may be an ineffective or damaging tactic for winning favor and approval.

DISCUSSION OF CONFORMITY
AND SELF-PRESENTATION RESULTS

The results give abundant testimony to the importance of the status variable in determining the content of self-reflecting communications in a well-defined hierarchy. The major question which arises in attempting to interpret the various differences in behavior associated with status, is whether or not these differences are systematically affected by ingratiation pressures. In other words, while there is clear evidence that both the independent variables of status and ingratiation-control context were determinants of communicative responses, it is not nearly as clear that the ingratiation instructions gave rise to different interpersonal tactics as a function of status.

The most novel and intriguing feature of the conformity data would seem to be the variations captured by the statistical interaction between status and issue relevance. Especially in the ingratiation condition, there was a clear tendency for HS subjects to conform less on relevant than on irrelevant issues. As noted above, this finding fits in with the notion that leaders must maintain the respect of their followers in order to be effective, but they must also find some means of demonstrating their approachability. It is perhaps not too surprising that HS subjects were able to resist influence on the Navy items, but what is rather remarkable is the extent to which they conformed on the less relevant, miscellaneous issues.

The extent of social influence on the miscellaneous items was definitely a function of the ingratiation instructions. The HS subjects under control instructions showed significantly less conformity on these issues than those under ingratiation instruction ($F = 6.69, p < .03$). Because of the amount of conformity in the ingratiation condition, and the significant reduction in the control condition, we may conclude that agreement on issues irrelevant to the status hierarchy served for HS subjects as a means of increasing their attractiveness, that is, their approachability. The fact that HS subjects also showed slightly less conformity on the Navy items in the control condition ($F = 2.29$, $p = ns$) does not seriously qualify this conclusion, though it suggests that the leader's attempt to increase approachability may even involve some conformity on issues related to the hierarchy.

In marked contrast to HS subjects, LS subjects in the ingratiation condition showed greatest conformity on those issues most relevant to the hierarchy. Undoubtedly, some of this differential conformity on high-relevance items may be attributed to the direct or informational effects of being exposed to an "expert's" opinions. The assumption here would be that HS subjects were perceived to be more knowledgeable (relative to LS subjects) about life in the Navy than about such an issue as the contribution of comic books and crime movies to the rise in juvenile delinquency (one of the miscellaneous items). This assumption seems plausible. In addition to the direct effects of expertise on the differential conformity of LS subjects, however, ingratiation instructions also made a contribution. Thus LS subjects conformed significantly more under ingratiation instructions on both Navy issues ($F = 4.08, p < .05$) and miscellaneous issues ($F = 6.85, p < .01$).

In dealing with the joint effects of relevance and ingratiation pressures on conformity, it is pertinent to consider an important conceptual distinction which has been introduced, and periodically reintroduced, into theoretical analyses of social influence processes. This is the distinction between direct and reflected comparison (Gerard, 1961). Direct social comparison involves reliance upon another as an impersonal mediator of certain facts about reality. Reflected social comparison occurs when an individual conforms in order to achieve some interpersonal goal (such as praise or acceptance) rather than solely to have his opinions coincide with what now appears to be a correct view of reality.

The ingratiation instructions in the present experiment presumably increase the amount of influence pressure based on the reflected component without changing the contribution of the direct comparison component. The HS subject remains better informed about Naval matters than the LS subject, regardless of the induced variations in dependence. We may conclude that the significant main effect of the ingratiation instructions on the general level of conformity behavior represents this increment stemming from reflected comparison. On the other hand, the pattern of interaction between issue relevance and status does not shift significantly as a function of ingratiation versus control instructions. While status-related changes as a function of relevance are monotonic only under ingratiation instructions, the most conservative conclusion is that direct comparison largely determines the greater *differential* conformity on the relevant Navy items. Thus while reflected comparison seems to have much to do with the general level of conformity behavior in both status groups, variations as a function of issue relevance are more likely to be determined by the subjects' judgment of the validity of the information received. Whether or not these specific conclusions are supported by additional research, the significant simple interaction between status and relevance is a provocative finding, one which is of interest both for practical and theoretical reasons.

With respect to the self-presentation data, HS subjects always presented themselves more favorably on important than on unimportant attributes, but they became significantly more modest on both kinds of attributes when under instructions to be ingratiating. As the argument was developed above, the greater favorability of self-presentation on important versus unimportant traits seems quite consistent with the presumed interest of the leader in emphasizing certain strong points to gain respect and certain weaknesses to increase approachability. This tendency was slightly (and not significantly) greater after ingratiation than after control instructions. The general tendency to become more self-deprecating on both kinds of items is clearly the more striking feature of the data for HS subjects in the ingratiation condition. This is certainly compatible with the notion of a greater concern with approachability in this condition, though it is not clear why the HS subjects show a slight tendency to deprecate themselves on important traits as well as on unimportant ones.

The LS subjects were similar to the HS subjects in rating themselves less favorably on the important items in the ingratiation versus the control condition. However, in striking departure from the high-status "modesty" effect, LS subjects' ratings of unimportant attributes were significantly more positive in the ingratiation than in the control condition. A possible explanation for the ratings in this condition involves assuming that a certain amount of defensiveness characterizes the behavior of a low-status person when it is important that he be liked or accepted by a high-status person. We may expand on Blau's (1960) reasoning to argue that a low-status person cannot advertise his weaknesses without endangering his reputation as a valuable team member, and to suggest that a person in a weak position who further emphasizes his personal failings arouses a certain embarrassment in others and thereby makes himself less attractive.

This might explain what happens on the unimportant items, but what of the reverse trend on the important items? Why did LS subjects become more self-effacing on these items when under pressure to make themselves more attractive? The answer may lie in the subtle understanding, even by freshmen, of the dynamics of leader-follower relations. The low-status person who describes himself very favorably on important personal attributes may be viewed as a presumptive upstart, one who may annoy the leader by usurping some of the characteristics of the leader's role. It may be, then, that LS subjects lowered their self-evaluations on important items because they wanted to avoid the appearance of claiming leadership qualities and, thereby, of threatening the leader's authority. In the ingratiation condition, the result is an equalization of favorability on different sorts of items: relative to their self-presentations under control conditions, LS subjects were more modest in rating their important characteristics and more immodest in rating their less important ones.

The study by Jones, Gergen, and Jones (1963) was planned to maximize the likelihood of discovery, rather than to assure the confirmation or disconfirmation of rigorously derived predictions. It is hardly surprising, then, that the results do not provide firm answers to theoretical questions concerning the interaction between status differences and ingratiation pressures. To mention a few of the shortcomings of the study, a number of relevant control comparisons were lacking (such as communication between two LS or two HS subjects), the variable of status was obviously a conglomerate of different age-related factors buttressed by experimental assignment, the dimension of relevance was very crudely defined in a priori empirical terms, the pattern of incoming messages introduced a constant but rather unique social stimulus, and the sequence of messages was not counter-balanced. Nevertheless, the results of the study do raise a number of intriguing questions and point in the direction of more clearly defined hypotheses for future study.

The second experiment to be reported in this chapter focused on the plight of the low-status person and was an attempt to reach back further into the motivational conditions underlying the decision to ingratiate. While the Jones, Gergen, and Jones (1963) study led the subjects by rather pointed instructions to the very brink of the ingratiation decision, the study by Jones, Gergen, Gumpert, and Thibaut (in press) was less directive or constraining in its arousal procedures. We attempted to create a performance situation in which subjects were not merely instructed to create an attractive impression, but in which all other avenues of improving their pessimistic condition were effectively ruled out by experimental arrangement. We were thus concerned, in the second study, more with whether ingratiation would occur in response to a theoretically appropriate set of motivational conditions, than with the form that ingratiation would take given strong role demands. Nevertheless, the second experiment was designed to make it possible to derive the form of ingratiation from specific information about the target person. Rather than treating the characteristics of the target person as a constant, as in the previous experiment, his characteristics were systematically varied to enable more precise predictions about the vicissitudes of conformity, self-presentation, and other-enhancement.

AN EXPERIMENT ON THE USE OF INGRATIATION TO INFLUENCE PERFORMANCE EVALUATION

In chapter one an attempt was made to fit the concept of ingratiation into Thibaut and Kelley's (1959) exchange-of-outcomes model. It was there proposed that ingratiation can be viewed as a set of strategies designed to equalize power in a relationship. The low-power person may maintain his outcomes at an acceptable level by complying with the wishes or directives of the high-power person. If we translate these abstract variations of power into the concrete terms of a worker-supervisor relationship, the worker may gain his rewards by performing in line with task criteria defined by the supervisor. While the supervisor is in a position to move the worker through a wide range of outcomes, the worker may, through effective task performance, narrow the range of outcomes received to those at the positive end of the potential span of outcomes. In so doing he would "verify" the predictive structure of the outcome matrix and fall in with its implications of differential power. In line with the values in the task-relevant matrix, the worker would be exchanging his labor or services for equitable rewards.

While the worker may thus effectively exert counter-power through his own activities within the task system, this means of control may not be available or attractive to him. A worker who lacks appropriate talent might be unable to meet the supervisor's standards, or those standards might themselves be so ambiguous that *he* could deliver in the interaction. While the ineffective stances, we might expect to find the worker attempting to control the supervisor by illicit maneuvers outside the task system itself. These maneuvers might be designed ultimately to increase the worker's relative power by increasing his attractiveness as a person and thereby enhancing the value of rewards and punishments that *he* could deliver in the interaction. While the ineffective or bewildered worker might attempt to present himself in a positive manner to bias the supervisor in his favor, this would effectively increase the worker's outcomes only if the supervisor were himself uncertain about good and bad performances or if he were free to choose among competing standards in evaluating a complex task. This is an instance, then, in which the decision of the worker to ingratiate himself with the supervisor would be conditioned by his understanding that his overtures (x) would be likely to result in the favorable treatment (y) desired.

The Jones, Gergen, Gumpert, and Thibaut (in press) experiment was an attempt to demonstrate that ingratiation will occur when a worker feels that it will be difficult to improve his outcomes within the task system itself, and when he is led to believe that the supervisor has some freedom to develop and modify his standards of performance evaluation. The first condition has to do with the incentive value of y, since outcomes controlled by the supervisor are presumably more gratifying or important when it is difficult to secure them by normal task performance activities. The second condition involves the subjective probability of x leading to y—the supervisor must not be constrained by his role in such a way that he is immune to influence. The experiment also attempted to show that the form the worker's ingratiating acts take will be determined by his impression of the supervisor's values and personal vulnerabilities.

Having thus set the stage and introduced the players, we may now consider in more detail the problems and opportunities created in the present experiment. Picture a worker who has just been introduced to a rather vague, complex, and ambiguous task. The task involves a series of similar problems which he is required to solve on a trial-by-trial basis. He quickly learns that the problems are soluble, but his own prospects for solving them are clearly not good: a supervisor, whom he has only briefly met, provides a pattern of outcomes indicating the worker's poor performance over a series of practice problems. Through a plausible experimental arrangement, the worker is led into a controlled interaction with the supervisor. They exchange opinions about important and trivial issues, exchange self-ratings, and end up trading evaluative ratings of each other. This controlled interaction provides an opportunity for the worker to try to impress the supervisor if he is so inclined. What conditions are likely to entice the worker to put this opportunity to use?

As forecast by the foregoing discussion, the degree of supervisory freedom in developing and applying standards of evaluation seems critical. Thus, in the experiment the worker either learns that the supervisor is free to decide after each trial whether a solution is correct, or that he is committed to a series of problem solutions which he has worked out in advance. In the former case there exists a possibility of biasing the supervisor's decisions in the worker's favor; no such possibility exists in the latter case. The general prediction would be that ingratiation should occur when the supervisor is potentially open to influence but not when he is restricted to preestablished criteria in his decisions to reward or punish.

But if ingratiation does occur, what form is it likely to take and how may it be identified? Common experience suggests that ingratiation attempts occur when the prospects for success (that is, creating an attractive impression) outweigh the risks of failure. These prospects are determined both by the surrounding conditions of interaction and the apparent characteristics of the target person. Furthermore, the characteristics of the target person should actually shape the form of ingratiation once it occurs. In the present experiment, the worker received one of two patterns of preinformation about the supervisor's beliefs and values. The worker was either led to believe that the supervisor, in his leader role, especially valued togetherness, accommodation, and worker solidarity or that he was concerned only with effective performance and did not care about the frills of group cohesiveness and personal styles which contribute to it.

Knowing this much, we can predict some of the more likely variations in impression management as a function of the supervisor's openness to influence and his personal views about the leadership role. As in the previous experiment the major dependent variables of the present study were opinion conformity, self-presentation, and other-enhancement. The most confident prediction is that opinion conformity or agreement between worker and supervisor should be greatest when the latter is open to influence and he emphasizes the importance of human relations; least when the supervisor is open to influence but competence and performance are admired. Under the latter circumstances, a show of independence provides some evidence of competence through the associative relationship which presumably links competence to assertiveness and self-confidence. When the supervisor is not open to influence, conformity should be moderate and more in the nature of cognitive readjustment than instrumental opinion change.

The prediction with respect to self-presentation was not so clear. The most reasonable expectation was that those subjects exercising the ingratiation option would (a) show that they too valued whatever personal attributes were stressed by the supervisor and (b) attempt to convince the supervisor that they possessed these attributes in fair degree. While the first part of this prediction was open to a direct test (subjects were asked to check those attributes they considered important), the second part raised difficulties. It seems likely that blatant self-advertisement is not very winning as an ingratiation tactic, and it is difficult for a person to establish his affability or his competence through self-declaration alone. With trepidation, then, it was predicted that subjects would describe themselves more positively on attributes admired by the supervisor than on attributes belittled by him, and that this tendency would be especially strong when the supervisor was potentially open to influence.

With respect to the third dependent variable, other-enhancement, it was predicted that subjects in the open-to-influence conditions would be more favorable in their supervisor ratings than those in the closed conditions. This was expected to be especially true on those personal attributes known to be prized by the supervisor.

METHOD

The experimental procedures involved rather elaborate stage setting and each subject was exposed to a complicated sequence of events. A detailed account of these procedures is included in the original report of the experiment (Jones, Gergen,

Gumpert, and Thibaut, in press) and we shall restrict ourselves here to a brief overview of the procedural sequence.

A total of fifty male volunteers were recruited from the introductory psychology course at the University of North Carolina to participate in the experiment. They appeared for the experiment in pairs and were introduced to an experimental accomplice identified as a graduate student in the School of Business Administration. The subjects were informed that they were to be players in a game designed to simulate the features of a real business concern. The graduate student was to serve as the supervisor in the game. He was to evaluate the performance of the two subjects and to give or take away points accordingly.

The experimenter then explained that the period would be divided into three parts. First there was to be a practice session in which the subjects would learn how the game was played. Then there was to be a "get-acquainted" session in which the subjects and the supervisor would get to know each other a little better as persons. Finally, the game was to be played for points. While the final game was continually referred to as the climax of the experiment, the task toward which everything else was to lead, it was not actually played.

Variation in conditions of supervisory judgment.   All subject pairs were told that the supervisor had previously looked over relevant literature in preparation for his judging task. However, for approximately half of the pairs the experimenter emphasized both to the subjects and to the supervisor that the information was general in its implications and, he said, turning to the supervisor, "these materials . . . won't give you the specific information you need in order to evaluate the other's decisions in the game. You'll just have to wait until you hear each worker's answer each time, and then use your best judgment in awarding points." Because of the implied freedom of the supervisor to make on-the-spot decisions, this instructional variation will hereafter be called the Open Judgment, or merely *Open* condition.

The remaining subject pairs were told, on the other hand, that the materials which the supervisor had been studying prior to their arrival provided much of the data on which the answers could be based. In addition, subjects in this, the Closed Judgment or *Closed* condition were told, "He has already recorded his answers to each of the practice problems and also to each of the problems in the game to be played for real. . . . These will serve as the correct answers and each of your responses will be judged right or wrong in terms of whether they match the supervisor's sheet or not." After the Open or Closed variation had been induced, the supervisor was taken to an adjoining room to finish looking over the materials.

The subjects were then taken to individual booths and exposed in turn to a practice game, information about the supervisor's values, and the get-acquainted session.

Practice game. In the business game the task was to rank sets of advertising slogans in terms of their probable effectiveness in increasing sales for a designated product. By prearranged performance feedback, each subject was led to expect that he would do poorly in the actual game and that the other subject would do well.

Variation in supervisor's values. Prior to the get-acquainted message exchange, each subject listened over earphones to an (actually tape-recorded) interview of the supervisor by the experimenter. The interview probed the supervisor's values with respect to leadership in business and industry. Half of the subjects heard the supervisor emphasize the "human side" of business: the importance of morale, getting along with others, cooperation, and mutual supportiveness. In view of the emphasis on solidardity the supervisor in this condition is hereafter referred to as *Sol.* The remaining subjects were exposed to interview responses in which the supervisor stressed the quality and quantity of job performance above all else. In view of his emphasis on productivity, the supervisor in this condition is hereafter referred to as *Prod.*

Get-acquainted session. Each subject then engaged in a pseudo-interaction with the supervisor which was similar to that featured in the prior experiment with ROTC students. He completed in the same sequence a self-rating questionnaire to be transmitted to the supervisor, a shortened version of an opinion questionnaire he had completed earlier in the semester, and finally he rated the supervisor on the same questionnaire form used for the self-ratings. He was led to believe that the supervisor was filling out the opinion questionnaire while he, the subject, was rating himself; the supervisor was filling out his self-rating form while the subject was indicating his opinions; and both were evaluating each other during the final phase of the exchange.

The *self-rating form* consisted of twenty pairs of attributive antonyms, each to be rated on a twelve-point scale in terms of how the subject saw himself (actual ratings) and how he would like to see himself (ideal ratings). Half of the items were preselected to form a cluster of qualities connoting the presence of *affability* and warmth; the remainder were traits more clearly related to competence in performance and are hereafter designated as *respect* items.

The *opinion questionnaire* consisted of twenty items of heterogeneous content each separated by a twelve-point scale along which agreement or disagreement could be expressed. As he confronted the task of recording his opinions, each subject was exposed to ratings on the same opinions allegedly made by the supervisor. These incoming opinion messages had been predoctored by the experimenter so that the ratings agreed with the subject's preexperimental opinions on some items but disagreed rather markedly on others. (The pattern of agreement and disagreement was constant from subject to subject.)

The *other description form* was identical in appearance to the self-description rating form. The self and ideal scales were already filled in, presumably by the supervisor, and the subject was left with the task of evaluating the supervisor before the form was returned to the latter.

A *final questionnaire* was also administered to inquire into the subject's "private" impressions of the supervisor, his view of the experimental setting, and his awareness of opportunities for social influence. The subjects were then told that the experiment was completed, informed of the true purpose of the experiment and of the deceptions involved, and requested not to discuss the experiment with classmates. Each received two dollars for his cooperation.

RESULTS

Opinion conformity as an ingratiation tactic.   A major hypothesis of the business game study concerned the interactive impact of both independent variables on the degree to which subjects would conform to the supervisor's opinions. Specifically, it was predicted that subjects in the Open Judgment conditions would conform more to Sol and less to Prod than would subjects in the Closed conditions. As detailed above, conditions for estimating the degree of conformity were established by having the supervisor appear to transmit his own opinion ratings, some of which were systematically discrepant from the earlier expressed opinions of the subject. The subject was instructed to respond to each of the supervisor's opinions with his own.

In the ROTC study the measure of conformity was quite circumstantial and its validity rested on the reasonable assumption that the subject would have responded at or near the class norm in the absence of social influence. In the business game experiment there was a standardized discrepancy between the bogus incoming opinion ratings and the subject's own "before" score. One way of measuring the degree of conformity was to sum the ultimate discrepancies between the supervisor's and the subject's opinion ratings. Such an index was scored for each subject and though the results fell into the predicted pattern and approached significance, the variability was dismayingly great. Much of this variability probably reflected opinion changes occurring between the "before" measure and the beginning of the experiment, and it was possible for drastic changes on individual items to obscure the overall pattern of conformity or nonconformity. It was decided, therefore, to limit the contribution of individual opinion items and to assign each subject a score based on the frequency of his conformity as inferred by the direction of pre-post change. Disregarding the magnitude of this change, a score of one was assigned for each rating falling between the pre-rating and two points beyond the supervisor's rating; all other items were simply assigned a zero. The decision to include movement slightly beyond the supervisor's rating seemed psychologically reasonable and was an a priori decision. The choice of two points beyond, rather than one or three, was arbitrary. This method reduces substantially the within-cell variance and the predicted interaction is clearly significant (p. < .05). The means of this "movement index" are presented in Table 8, along with a summary of the analysis of variance.

TABLE 8——Opinion conformity: measure of movement toward supervisor

A. *Movement Index Means**

	JUDGMENT CONTEXT	
	OPEN	CLOSED
SOLIDARITY	8.9	6.9
PRODUCTIVITY	6.7	7.6

B. *Analysis of Variance Summary*

SOURCE	df	MS	F
OPEN-CLOSED	1	.31	
SOL-PROD	1	.57	
INTERACTION	1	2.09	5.08†
ERROR	35	.41	

* The higher the score, the greater the incidence of movement toward the supervisor. For each subject, each of the 20 discrepant items was assigned a score of +1 for movement toward the supervisor and a zero otherwise.

† p <.05.

Favorability of self-presentation. Prior to the exchange of opinion messages, subjects were instructed to describe themselves to the supervisor via a twenty-item rating scale composed of evaluative personal attributes in antonym form. The content of these attributes had been preselected so that half of them connoted qualities relevant to judgments of respect or admiration for personal strength and competence (respect items) while the remaining half centered around qualities of friendliness and approachability (affability items). The apparent congruence between these two categories of item content and the qualities emphasized by the two supervisors was, of course, deliberately contrived. It was expected that the Open Judgment context would give rise to ingratiating self-presentations in the particular areas stressed as important by the subject's supervisor.

It will be recalled that subjects both rated themselves and indicated their ideal position on each antonym. They were also instructed to check attribute-pairs they considered especially important in determining the attractiveness of others. As mentioned in our introduction to this study, the expectation was that those subjects in the Open conditions would show that they too valued whatever personal attributes were stressed by the supervisor. The most direct means to this end was, presumably, for the subject to attach more importance to these attributes.

Considering the results, Sol subjects did emphasize the importance of affability items whereas Prod subjects attached more importance to respect items ($P_{diff} = .01$). While this differential emphasis was more marked in the Open treatments, the interaction between judgment condition and supervisor values was not significant. This outcome suggests that the subjects' conceptions of important attributes were shaped by the supervisor's comments during the interview, but there was no clear evidence that the subjects used agreement with the supervisor's standards to win his favor.

The remaining issue concerns evidence that the subjects in the Open conditions tried to convince the supervisor that they in fact possessed the admired attributes. It was predicted that subjects would describe themselves more positively on attributes admired by the supervisor than on attributes ignored or belittled by him, and that this tendency would be especially strong when the supervisor was potentially open to influence. This prediction was proposed with some hesitance in view of the fact that a person, for example, does not necessarily convince others that he is noble by constantly extolling his own nobility. But the studies by Jones, Gergen, and Davis (1962) and by Gergen (1962) showed that female subjects became more self-enhancing when instructed to create a good impression. In the study by Jones, Gergen, and Jones (1963) which has just been summarized, low-status ROTC students became more self-enhancing when instructed to win the favor of higher-status students, except on those items judged to be especially important. Because of the variation of perceived item importance as a function of experimental treatment in the present study, the effects of importance on self-ratings could not be meaningfully studied.

Table 9 presents the mean values of both self and ideal ratings on respect and affability attributes; the lower the value, the closer the self or ideal rating to the positive or favorable end of the scale. Several features of this rather complex table deserve comment. First of all, there is no reliable tendency for subjects to describe themselves favorably on all items or on affability items as a function of either judgmental context or supervisor values. When the analysis is restricted to respect attributes, however, there is a strong effect of the Sol-Prod variable on both self and ideal ratings. When confronted with a supervisor who has previously emphasized performance and competence, subjects locate their ideal selves closer to the scale extremes represented by such trait names as efficient, original, well organized, and level-headed. In addition, they present themselves as actually having more of these characteristics when communicating to Prod.

While these systematic variations in respect to item ratings are of interest in their own right, reflecting as they do an implicit tailoring of the presented self to accommodate the characteristics of another, there is no evidence in the raw data of Table 9 that this accommodation served as an ingratiation tactic. That is, the subjects' tendency to model themselves after the

TABLE 9——Favorability of self-presentation (self and ideal ratings on respect and affability attributes)

EXPERIMENTAL CONDITION

		OPEN		CLOSED		Significant Comparisons
		Sol	Prod	Sol	Prod	
AFFABILITY	SELF	35.64	38.50	37.18	33.60	—
	IDEAL	21.91	25.00	25.63	25.00	—
RESPECT	SELF	39.91	34.86	47.00	35.40	S vs P: p <.01
	IDEAL	22.09	15.86	25.00	16.20	S vs P: p <.001
TOTAL	SELF	75.55	73.36	84.18	69.00	—
	IDEAL	44.00	40.86	50.63	41.20	—
RESPECT-AFFABILITY DISCREPANCY*		4.27	—3.64	9.82	1.80	S vs P: p <.01 O vs C: p <.05
SELF-IDEAL DISCREPANCY						
	AFFABILITY	13.73	13.50	11.55	8.60	—
	RESPECT	17.82	19.00	22.00	19.20	—
R — A†		4.09	5.50	10.27	10.60	O vs C: p <.05

* The lower the score the greater the tendency to describe self positively on respect (relative to affability) items.

† The lower the score the greater the tendency to describe self (relative to ideal) positively on respect (relative to affability) items.

supervisor seems no greater in the Open than in the Closed conditions.

A notable (if unavoidable) weakness in the present design is its "after-only" nature. The final ratings of self and ideal are a compound of current subjective state, self-conscious strategy, scale interpretation, and other sources of idiosyncratic response bias. This is probably the reason why there is such excessive variability in the self-presentation scores. In an effort to get a clearer picture of the experimental effects less contaminated by these sources of response bias, the following procedure was adopted as a way of using each subject as his own control. Since there were no systematic differences in either self or ideal ratings on affability items, and since affability self-ratings were moderately correlated with respect self-ratings (r's ranging from .431 to .784), each subject was assigned a score representing favorable self-rating on respect items minus favorable self-rating on affability items. The resulting R-A difference score serves as an index of the subject's tendency to describe himself positively on respect relative to affability items. This provides a relative emphasis score and also controls for each subject's tendency to restrict himself to a particular region of the scale.

Placing these R-A scores in a factorial design yields two significant main effects: the Sol-Prod variation is highly significant and judgmental context has a reliable effect (see Table 9). Thus not only do subjects show a general tendency to place a relative stress on their respect-worthy qualities when confronted with a task-oriented, performance-centered supervisor; they also stress respect qualities when they are in a position to influence the supervisor to act in their behalf.

A final point needs to be considered before leaving the self-presentation results. It has been noted that both self and ideal ratings on respect items were clearly affected by the supervisor's characteristics. This suggests that the Sol-Prod variable influenced in a general way the manner in which the scale should be used, but it did not affect the relative placement of self and ideal ratings. It is as if the supervisor, through his interview responses, defined for the subject what is "good"—it is good to be extremely competent, strong, and cool-headed, for example—but he did not affect the manner in which the subject saw himself relative to maximal goodness. The Open-Closed variable, on the other hand, did affect this placement of self relative to ideal so that subjects presented themselves as more competent, and so forth, when more strongly motivated (in the Open conditions) to impress the supervisor with their worthiness.

This reasoning is supported by the last row of Table 9, which shows a final self-ideal discrepancy index. Since the effects of shifting both self and ideal ratings cancelled each other out, only the Open-Closed variable remained significant.

It should be emphasized that the obtained pattern of self-presentation results was not predicted in detail. In particular, there was at the outset no theoretical reason to expect systematic variations in respect items but not affability items. It is also clear that the Open-Closed variable had weak effects on most indices of self-presentation, reaching substantial proportions only with a derived index of self-enhancement on respect minus affability items. Nevertheless, the significant findings reported are provocative, and their implications will be discussed below.

Other-enhancement.   As in the ROTC study, the final portion of the interchange between subjects and supervisor involved ratings of the supervisor on the same sheet on which the supervisor had presumably rated himself. These ratings were to be transmitted to the targets of evaluation. In the earlier study, low-status subjects showed a tendency to evaluate their high-status partners more positively in the ingratiation than in the control condition; no such differential tendency was observed in the analogous conditions of the present study. That is, contrary to experimental expectations, subjects in the Open conditions were not more favorable in their transmitted ratings of the supervisor than subjects in the Closed conditions. Nor were there any more subtle effects depending on the content of the items. Rating variability was extremely high, and it may be that the experimental inductions had lost their potency by the time the "other ratings" took place.

DISCUSSION

The prediction that conformity would be greatest in the Open-Sol condition and least in the Open-Prod condition was confirmed, though it is clear from an inspection of the means that the Open-Sol treatment was the main contributor to the significant interaction. The theoretical interpretation of the predicted interaction assumes that subjects in both Open conditions have a special concern with being liked or admired, but that they must implement this concern in different ways. Subjects in the Open-Sol condition are invited by circumstances and the nature of the target to employ conformity for strategic purposes. Subjects in the Open-Prod condition, on the other hand, are confronted with a person who seems to devalue opinion agreement as such and circumstances seem to point away from conformity as a tactic for impressing the supervisor. Some interesting, if tentative, correlational data seem to support this interpretation. Those subjects who express an interest in being attractive to the supervisor (as measured by a series of items on the post-experimental questionnaire) show a special tendency to respond differently as a function of the supervisor's expressed values. In the Sol conditions, the correlation between conformity and attraction motivation was .434; in the Prod conditions the correlation between the same two variables was $-.179$. In spite of the small samples involved, the difference between these correlations is almost significant ($p < .10$), suggesting that wanting to be liked leads to conformity only when the target person himself seems to value accommodation and togetherness. With a few qualifications, then, the results fit the argument developed in the introductory section: the openness of supervisory judgment provides the incentive to concentrate on creating an attractive impression; the supervisor's own emphasis on effective interpersonal relations points out the appropriate path of impression management.

The tenuous but provocative self-presentation results also merit some discussion. It is apparent that self-descriptions on traits connoting interpersonal warmth and congeniality were unaffected by the experimental variables. Ideal ratings on these traits were similarly unaffected. This is quite surprising in view of the Solidarity supervisor's explicit emphasis on the value and importance of such traits in work groups. In comparison, the stated values of the supervisor had a clear effect on ratings of traits connoting competence and personal power. Both self-descriptions and ideal ratings were more favorable in the Productivity conditions. The fact that both sets of ratings were more positive suggests that respect attributes are evaluated relative to a shifting standard, a standard quite sensitive to the value attached to competence and performance by a supervisor. Self and ideal evaluations on affability attributes may be more firmly anchored in each individual's past experiences with others. Many subjects may have entered the experimental situation with the conviction that too much friendliness and warmth is a bad thing and this conviction was little influenced by the promptings of the Solidarity supervisor.

Of greater theoretical interest was the tendency for subjects in the Open conditions to present themselves as closer to their ideal on respect than on affection items—relative to the subjects in the Closed conditions. For whatever reason, subjects in the Open conditions were more anxious to impress the supervisor with their competence than their affability. Under the circumstances, if the supervisor could be led to have respect for the subject's judgment, he might begin to assign more points for the latter's solution attempts. Such an increase in respect could, of course, have no such effect in the Closed conditions. Impressing the Open Judge with one's competence seems to be a more direct way to influence his judgment than presenting oneself as affable.

The expectation that subjects in the Open conditions would flatter the supervisor—especially on those attributes he has stressed as valuable—was not confirmed by the data. It may be true that rating the supervisor in a complimentary way is viewed as a risky or inopportune strategy of influence, a conclusion that we would more readily accept were it not for the results of the preceding experiment. In our considered judgment, however, the Open-Closed induction had probably lost much of its strength before the final rating scales were administered. Not only had a fair amount of time elapsed since the instructions had emphasized this variable, but there probably were growing suspicions that the "real" game would never be played. Apropos of this suggestion —that the induction had lost its strength by the time subjects were asked to rate their supervisors—there is evidence in the post-experimental questionnaire that at least in the crucial Open-Sol condition, those who remained interested in making themselves attractive *did* evaluate the supervisor more positively. Only in the Open-Sol condition did a questionnaire measure of attractiveness motivation show a firm positive correlation with favorability of ratings ($r = .636$); in the other conditions the correlation between the same two indexes ranged from $-.131$ to $+.082$. Perhaps if the Open-Judgment induction had been stronger, the former correlation would have been lower and the tendency for subjects in the Open-Solidarity condition to flatter would have been more uniform.

SUMMARY AND CONCLUSIONS

In the present chapter we have presented the results of two experiments designed to illuminate some of the vicissitudes of impression management within a hierarchy of differential status or power. The concept of power is inextricably woven into the fabric of ingratiation, since the tactical pursuit of approval must have some motivational basis in a desire for approval-mediated resources. And yet, to say that one member of a dyad has less power in general than the other, is not to say that the other has no occasion to be ingratiating, for he has his own areas of dependence on the subordinate. While ingratiation upwards in a hierarchy is burdened by the fact that the low-status person's relative deprivation is transparent, ingratiation downwards involves its own subtleties. Proceeding from an intuitive analysis of the psychological positions of low- and high-status ingratiators, an experiment was designed to explore those tactical responses to the conditions of dependence which might be a function of the dependent person's general status. Experimentally induced pressures to make an attractive impression led all subjects to show greater opinion conformity to the target, led the high-status subjects to become more modest in describing themselves, and the low-status subjects to become more favorable in their ratings of the target. With the exception of the latter result, the pattern of findings was consistent with our general expectations. The low-status person presented himself in an agreeable and rather undifferentiated way, playing down his strengths in important areas and concealing his weaknesses in less important ones. The high-status person revealed in his behavior a concern with making himself approachable without undercutting his own high position, and he did this primarily by presenting a modest face on unimportant self-attributes and an agreeing posture on issues which were not relevant to his claims for superior status in the ROTC.

The second experiment concentrated on the communications of the low-status person in a supervised task setting, and attempted to show that ingratiating overtures will occur when the higher-status supervisor is free to modify his behavior in ways which might affect the ingratiator's rewards, that is, when the supervisor is open to influence. The form of this ingratiation was expected to hinge on the expressed values of the supervisor. The results showed that opinion conformity was affected by the supervisor's stated values and that this was true only when the supervisor was potentially open to influence. Also, in the open-to-influence conditions the subjects tried to impress the supervisor by presenting themselves as strong and competent. There was no evidence of differential flattery as a function of experimental treatment. Perhaps the most important feature of the second experiment is that the findings provide support for the model of determinants developed in chapter four. It is not the sheer fact of being low in power which gives rise to the initiation of impression-managing strategies. The high-power target person must also be in a position to give or withhold the desired resource as a function of his general attitude toward the low-power person. The subjective probability of x leading to y must be substantially greater than zero. An additional requirement which may be inferred is that the low-power person must find closed or too costly the more legitimate avenues of exerting counter-power through effective task performance.

6 Cognitions and Reactions of the Target Person

As noted in chapter one, the study of ingratiation requires separate consideration of the perspectives of two actors in a social interchange. Thus far we have emphasized the ingratiator's psychological position and have considered the target person and his position primarily from the ingratiator's point of view. We will now inquire into the target person's perspective and examine the conditions which affect his reactions to the ingratiator. In changing our focus we have considerable information on which to build, since much of the ground already covered in the preceding section could now merely be stated in the obverse. It seems reasonable to assume, for example, that the same social conditions which increase p's subjective probability estimate of success will lead o to respond favorably to an ingratiation attempt. This assumption would be valid at least to the extent that o and p perceive the basic features of the situation in a similar way. In laying out some of the conditions under which p thinks ingratiation will be successful, in other words, we have also laid out the conditions in which he will, in fact, succeed.

Rather than belabor many of the same points from the complementary position of the target person, the present section will emphasize o's motives, feelings, and cognitions and attempt to explore some special conditions governing his overt response. Separation of the psychological positions of p and o becomes especially important when we realize that p may systematically

161

misjudge the internal state of o both before and after his ingratiation attempt, and that p and o may indeed be responsive to quite different features of the same social setting. Our first goal is to show that the factors which shape the behavioral reaction of the target person are not necessarily the same as those which shape his internal condition, a state of affairs which makes it difficult for p to comprehend fully the effects of his behavior.

The immediate, overt response of o. How does the average person respond when he is profusely complimented? When another person slavishly agrees with his expressed opinions? When an unsolicited benefit is received from one who is dependent on him? While the precise nature of his reaction would be difficult to forecast, the average target of such potentially ingratiating gestures is likely to make some sign of gratitude or pleasure, often accompanied by an embarrassed disclaimer. The reaction may be a straightforward and noncommittal "thank you for the compliment." The ingratiator's benign intentions may be acknowledged with some such response as, "you're very kind," which again avoids any reference to the truth value of the compliment received. It is equally common for the truth value of an ingratiating comment to be questioned, along with an appreciative phase or gesture. Thus we often hear, "it's very flattering of you to say that," which carries more the implication of modest disclaimer than accusation of deceit. Or the target person may say "you are too kind," or, "you shouldn't have done it"—again statements questioning the validity of the exchange but clearly implying an acknowledgment of benevolent or generous motivation.

There are occasions, of course, where the validity of an evaluation is directly challenged and where o points out to p that the latter has missed a flaw or exaggerated an asset. Even in such cases, however, the motives of the potential ingratiator are rarely openly questioned. The important common feature of the vast majority of reactions to positive gestures from others is the communication of appreciation for their benevolent intentions. What may be crassly instrumental flattery is thus publicly interpreted as well-intentioned or normative flattery if it is not accepted as a matter of course. This is clearly an example of protective face-work (Goffman, 1955), since the target person commits himself to saving the face of the ingratiator. Regardless of what he really thinks of p's intentions, o is to an important extent bound by the face-work contract to avoid taking umbrage at p's overtures. One of the most interesting implications of this fact is that p usually receives immediate positive reinforcement for his ingratiating overtures, or at least he is not apt to be exposed to clear signals of negative reinforcement. Thus p is not in a good position to receive precise immediate feedback on the success of his attempt to bias o in his favor, and the rather ambiguous positive feedback he does receive may serve to perpetuate his tendency to ingratiate until he obtains more unequivocal evidence of his success or failure. Consideration of this last point leads us directly into the useful distinction between o's immediate behavioral reaction to ingratiation and changes in his underlying disposition to benefit p.

Responses mediated by changes in the motive state of o. While the immediate behavioral reaction to flattery is largely determined by well-internalized cultural norms, we have argued that the true goal of the flatterer is to bring about a favorable change in the target person's attitudes and feelings about him. As we have just argued, this change in internal state may be quite imperfectly reflected in overt behavior—at least in the short run. Junior executive p may notice that his ingratiating overtures elicit responses of pleasure and gratitude from his superordinate o, but he may also discover that he is no longer invited to o's house for informal gatherings and that his promotion has been overlooked. Thus we start with the contention that changes in o's attitudes toward p are often not readily apparent, and that boomerang effects in the attitudinal realm may be accompanied by polite and courteous consumption of compliments at the behavioral level.

Focusing on o's cognitive and motivational state, we may see that his major problem is one of inferring p's intentions. Because ingratiation attempts are seldom blatant, we might expect o to have complex cognitions and ambivalent affects when he attempts to sort out his impression of p. On the positive side, o may recognize that by his ingratiating efforts p acknowledges o's importance and value to him. ("We love flattery even though we are not deceived by it, because it shows that we are of importance enough to be courted." Emerson, *Essays, Second Series: Gifts*, quoted in Stevenson, 1934, p. 677.) In addition, *p* gives evidence of noncompetitive deference to *o* and makes remote any possibility of embarrassing him with public criticism. He appeals to *o*'s desire to believe the best about himself, and it is always possible that *p* is not only sincere but correct in his positive evaluation. On the negative side, to the extent that *o* questions the intentions behind *p*'s behavior, he loses confidence in the validity of any information which comes from *p*. He may dislike *p* merely because his saccharine comments force *o* into postures of modest self-deprecation, or leave him with no appropriate response. Undoubtedly there are many other affective subtleties which complicate *o*'s internal state even further. Nevertheless, it is proposed that *o*'s internal reaction can be classified along a rough dimension ranging from attraction-centered attitude changes to distrust-centered changes.

If we exploit a blend of logic, intuition, and informal observation, it is possible to identify roughly five clusters of "internal response" along this affective (trust-like, mistrust-dislike) dimension:

Cluster 1 involves the combination of *affection, affiliation, attraction,* and generally the unambivalent disposition to benefit *p*, to give him the benefit of all doubts, and to be biased in his favor. If *p* succeeds in inducing changes in attitude in this direction, we would say he has been eminently successful in his attempts to be ingratiating with *o*.(There are obviously other ways to induce such a change in attitude, but we are concerned here only with *p* as ingratiator and *o* as target person.)

Cluster 2 involves primarily subjective *feelings of restitution.* Here *o*'s positive feelings are somewhat more alloyed than in cluster 1, and tensions of obligation tend to break into awareness. As long as *o* feels very attracted to *p*, such tensions are muted or submerged. Where attraction is less extreme, however, the desire to benefit or to approve may be blended with the moral feeling that it should be done. Feelings of restitution emerge primarily out of *p*'s success in exploiting the norms of distributive justice as these affect o. Presumably feelings of restitution are more unstable and involve a more limited time span than feelings of attraction. If the benefit p seeks is a fairly self-contained y, o's provision of this y should discharge the tension of obligation and restore o's feelings of equity and interpersonal balance. But if y is impossible or difficult for o to produce, or if p is expected to continue to exploit distributive justice norms with new xs, feelings of restitution may be converted either into increased attraction or hostility and avoidance. In the former case, it would be as though o were trapped into friendship by his own tension-reducing benevolence to p. Dissonance theory alerts us to the possibility that benevolent behavior initiated by feelings of restitution might eventually be justified by an increase in o's attraction for the recipient of his good acts. This would be a more likely outcome if o found it difficult to leave the relationship for one or another reason. If the relationship were purely voluntary, and alternative relationships were available, we would expect o to respond to repeated xs which represent a minimally acceptable exchange for the desired ys with increasing resentment and private feelings of hostility.

Cluster 3 might be described in terms of *feelings of toleration* and *forbearance*. Such feelings are the minimally desired outcomes of one who flatters for defensive or self-protective reasons. Attraction and genuine affection are not likely to be involved in such cases for the forbearing reaction is more likely to be tinged with pity, or even a kind of patronizing scorn. O responds to p's suppliant overtures by adhering to an implicit contract to inhibit hostile, threatening behavior. The contract may extend to the protection of p from other sources of threat as well. The affective tone may vary, but would typically include feelings of nurturance, superiority, and tolerant disdain.

The remaining two clusters involve reactions sufficiently negative to qualify as boomerang effects.

Cluster 4 is heavily weighted with *feelings of embarrassment, annoyance,* and a strong disposition to avoid further interaction with p. In this case there is a marked disjunction between o's private feelings and his public response to p. Part of his desire to avoid p stems from the emotional strain of perpetuating this disjunction, or of not being able to act in a manner consonant with his private feelings.

While it is extremely difficult for most people to react to flattery and ingratiation with overt hostility, this remains a logical possibility and suggests that if there is an empirical *cluster 5*, it involves *feelings of disgust, moral indignation,* and a strong disposition toward reprisal. In this case, the negative or boomerang response is so strong that the silent contract of mutual face-saving is broken, and the unsuccessful ingratiator becomes the target of some damaging reaction. We would insist, however, that direct confrontation is exceedingly rare and that the reprisal is likely to be indirect and delayed. Obsequious flatterers are often discussed critically behind their backs, but rarely subjected to open criticism for their flattering manner.

These clusters give some idea of the range of effects attendant upon ingratiation and flattery. In a sense this range defines the nature of the risks entertained by the flatterer, quite independent of his own internal reactions of guilt or qualms of conscience. As we have emphasized in the preceding chapters, the risks are minimized, and the conscience is more easily stilled, when p is able to establish or use contextual cues which reveal or obscure motivational intent. As a way of summarizing o's reactions to p as a joint function of p's behavior and the context in which it occurs, we next turn to a useful schematic model of the reaction process.

A model of reactions to ingratiation.   As has been dismayingly obvious, the word ingratiation refers to a wide and varied range of social responses. Their only common feature is the intent to win attraction from a specific target person and thereby increase his disposition to favor, approve, or benefit the ingratiator. Beyond this description of intent, we may isolate certain common tactics but we will always be left with an incomplete list of the possible forms such attraction-oriented behavior can take. While it is clear that the motivational intent, rather than the specific behavioral form, is critical in the identification of ingratiation episodes, the form that such behavior takes is of obvious importance in generating predictions about effects. Some forms of ingratiating behavior will be more successful than others in eliciting attraction and avoiding hostility. It is also clear that the effectiveness of a given social overture is in part a function of the interaction context in which it occurs. A preliminary but important task is to organize the relevant classes of independent variables in a way that specifies testable functional relations with the dependent variable of the target person's internal reaction, and yet does this without anchoring these relations to particular forms of ingratiation.

The model depicted in Figure 4 attempts such a specification by considering (a) the frequency, consistency, and/or degree of

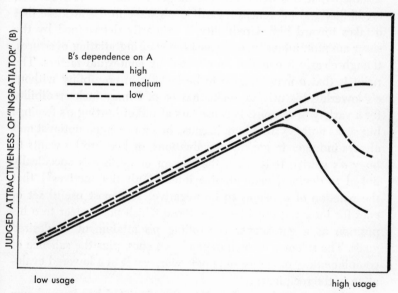

FIGURE 4——Theoretical relationship between use of ingratiation tactics and judged attractiveness of the ingratiator

tactical use and (b) the degree of dependence of p on o, as perceived by o. The target person's judgment of the ingratiator is expressed as a joint function of these two classes of variables. The figure is intended to be heuristic, and the particular form of the relationship depicted is to an extent arbitrary. Nevertheless, it is predicted that o's attraction for p increases throughout most of the range of using such instruments as compliments and conformity for gaining favor. It is also predicted that o's attraction will diminish under circumstances of extreme tactical use, and that this will be especially true when the ingratiator is obviously dependent on the target person.

The assumptions underlying this predicted family of curves are simple. As indicated above, the critical cognitive problem confronting o is that of determining p's motivational intent. It is assumed that this determination hinges on inferences regarding credibility and inferences regarding p's stake in the attitude that o takes toward him. Credibility is primarily determined by the sheer amount, intensity, and consistency of ingratiating overtures, though clearly it can also be affected by contextual factors. The point is that o may judge p to be lacking in credibility without o's lowering his private evaluation of p. P may lack credibility for a variety of reasons: because he's afraid of hurting o's feelings but seeks nothing from him, because he's a perennial optimist and always indulges in generous evaluations, or because he wants to buoy o's spirits. It is when the lack of credibility is specifically linked to devious, manipulative intent ("ulterior motives") that the reaction of o begins to be negative. The most useful set of cues for inferring this intent are those which make clear to o his position as a gatekeeper controlling p's attainment of desired goals. The salience of such dependence cues, plus the salience of complimentary or conforming behavior, result in a lowered evaluation in the recipient.

The general shape of the function depicted has been shown to hold both for the tactic of complimentary other-enhancement (Dickoff, 1961) and the tactic of conformity (Jones, Jones, and Gergen, 1963). We shall now describe the procedures and results of these two studies in some detail.

A STUDY OF REACTIONS TO EVALUATIONS BY ANOTHER PERSON

Dickoff (1961) was primarily interested in studying the responses of one person to varying evaluations of them made by others. There is solid empirical support for the proposition that, in general, we like those who evaluate us positively. The Dickoff study was designed to ask more precise questions about the following issues: Do we like those who agree with us about ourselves better than those who are uniformly positive in their evaluation? Does the answer to this question depend on the context in which this evaluation is delivered? Given the receipt of a positive evaluation or a more negative one, what is the role of a person's self-concept in his return ratings of the evaluator?

METHOD

In an attempt to answer these questions, Dickoff designed an experiment using seventy-eight female undergraduate subjects. Each subject was individually run through a session in which she presented a sample of behavior to an observer behind a one-way mirror. This behavior sample was elicited by a series of standard interview questions designed to reveal a fair amount about the subject's personal history, her manner, and her values in a short time. The observer behind the mirror allegedly recorded her impression of the subject. The two were then brought together and the subject was given the task of learning the impression which she had made on the observer. She did this by attempting to anticipate from a series of ninety-six trials or items, which of three attributes had been chosen to apply to herself. Each item consisted of a positive, a neutral, and a negative personal trait. The format of the items was very similar to that comprising the Triads Test in the study by Jones, Gergen, and Davis (1962) and were later modified to form the Self-Valuation Test used in Gergen's (1962) study. It was the subject's task to guess or predict which of these traits had been selected by the observer behind the mirror as applying to the subject.

Depending on the treatment to which the subject was arbitrarily assigned, the observer (an experimental accomplice) either responded with a uniformly positive evaluation (in other words the most positive attribute was always the correct choice for the subject), or her responses were identical to those made by the subject herself in an earlier group testing session, or the observer systematically avoided all positive attributes in favor of uniformly choosing the neutral one on each item. Thus the situation was one in which some subjects received an evaluation which was extremely positive and uniformly so, some subjects learned that the other person had very much the same impression of them that they had of themselves, and some learned that the other person had a rather evasive and, by implication, negative impression of them.

Cross-cutting these variations in evaluations received was a variation in instructional set. Those subjects operating under what we might call *accuracy* instructions were told that the specific purpose of the experiment was to discover "how accurately people form impressions of others." It was mentioned that the person behind the mirror would be "one of the first-year graduate students in clinical psychology, all of whom are participating in the study as part of their training." Parenthetically, it was indicated that in the training of clinical psychologists, an effort is made to help them be objective and prevent their own feelings from getting in the way of their judgments. The remainder of the subjects were given the *ulterior motive* instructions. These subjects were told that the purpose of the experiment was to determine how people form impressions of others. Again the observer was presented as a graduate student, but as one who had asked to take the place of the regular graduate assistant for the day. The rationale for her presence was that in exchange for serving as the observer she would like to be able to use the subject in an experiment of her own, following the present session. The experimenter explained that the observer would be very grateful for the subject's cooperation but that the decision was of course up to the subject. No mention was made of the importance of accuracy, but some vague remarks were made by the experimenter about her interest in the consistency of impressions. The intent of these instructions was to make the observer appear dependent on the subject's good will and to suggest that an ulterior motive might govern her relations with the subject.

The major dependent variable measure was a twenty-item rating scale on which each subject recorded her impression of the observer after having learned the observer's evaluation of her. Each item consisted of a descriptive statement about some personal characteristic followed by a seven-point scale on which the subject could indicate the degree of her agreement or disagreement with the scale. Eleven of the items had been selected to serve as an index of attraction both on a priori grounds and because they had discriminated highly in a group testing session prior to the experiment between ratings of a "liked" and a "disliked" person. Before filling out the rating scale, the subject was first asked to jot down her impression of the observer in her own words.

Since Dickoff was interested in tapping the subject's private feelings about the observer, insofar as this was possible, she (as experimenter) took pains to assure the subject that the subject's appraisal would not be seen by the observer. The subject was told to be as frank and honest as possible because it might come in handy for the experimenter to have a clear picture of various aspects of the experimental situation. By her manner and the wording of her request, the experimenter tried to convey the impression that the rating task was a fairly unimportant afterthought and that she would not be interested in using the subject's responses to evaluate the observer.

RESULTS

In the "learning task" itself, the subjects rapidly began to change their anticipations in the direction of the "concept" characterizing their particular treatment variation. That is, subjects in the *positive* conditions showed an increasing tendency to predict that the observer had chosen the positive characteristic in the up-coming triad as most characteristic of the subject. Those in the *neutral* condition showed a decreasing tendency to predict a choice of the positive characteristic, and those in the *self-concept* condition showed no change in this respect. The differences between the three feedback conditions in this kind of anticipation learning were highly significant, thus validating the manipulation of evaluative feedback. There were no discernible differences in the frequency of anticipating positive statements as a function of the interaction context (that is, *accuracy* versus *ulterior motive* instructions). However, subjects in the *accuracy* conditions later reported that they cared more about the impression they made than those in the *ulterior motive* treatments (t = 2.85, p < .01) and that they had tried harder to learn the observer's impression (t = 1.78, p < .10). There was other evidence, in the main results to be reported below, that the variation in feedback context was moderately effective, but only one subject (in the *ulterior motive positive* condition) indicated on a post-experimental questionnaire that the observer had engaged in flattery in order to elicit her assistance. Dickoff reports that the subjects were very involved in the anticipation learning task and that this high involvement was reflected in their obvious expressions of relief or disappointment when the conditions of the experiment were later revealed to them.

Dickoff's primary interest was in the subjects' ratings of the observer's dependence on the subject had an effect on attraction results are summarized in Figure 5, where the mean attraction scores are plotted for each of the six treatment combinations. Here it may be seen that there is a general relationship between the favorability of the evaluation received by the subject on the one hand, and the rating scale index of attraction for the observer on the other hand. It is especially clear that people respond in kind when they receive a relatively negative evaluation. As predicted by the model (see Figure 4), the instructions varying the observer's dependence on the subject had an effect on attraction when a uniform dose of positive evaluation was administered by the observer. It may be inferred by comparing the two *positive* condition means that high attraction begets high attraction as long as there is no reason to believe that the observer is motivated to be ingratiating.

A statistical comparison of the difference between mean attraction ratings of *accuracy positive* versus *ulterior motive positive* subjects shows that they are significantly different (t = 2.28, p < .05). Similarly, when the free impression sketches are rated for degree of attraction (with high inter-rater reliability), the

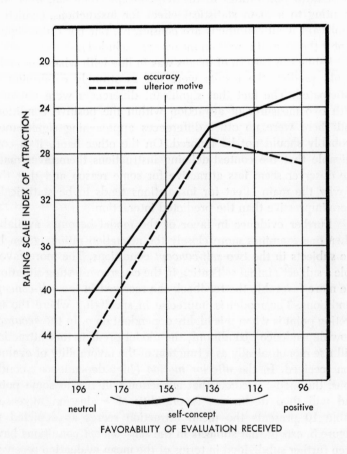

FIGURE 5——Mean rating scale attraction scores

same two conditions are again significantly different ($t = 2.07$, $p < .05$). The effects of evaluation context do not approach significance in either the self-concept or the neutral conditions. Unfortunately, however, with neither measure of attraction is there a significant interaction between the favorability of feedback received and the context within which it was delivered. The difficulty is that the *ulterior motive* instructions led to somewhat lower attraction ratings in the *self-concept* condition, thus contributing to a main statistical effect for instructions (which is significant if all conditions are considered, but not quite significant if the neutral condition means are excluded).

While the pattern of means was in line with what the model would predict, the results were not as strongly confirming as anticipated. The fact that significant differences were obtained with two measures of attraction within the positive conditions and there were no other differences approaching significance, probably should not be ignored. On the other hand, it is conceivable that the context-defining instructions themselves made the observer seem less attractive for some reason and that this is why the main effect for instructions tends to be statistically more impressive than the predicted interaction.

Further evidence in favor of the model becomes available when one examines more closely the attraction ratings given by the subjects in the two *self-concept* conditions. The more favorable a subject's initial self-rating in the classroom-testing situation, the more favorable the feedback she received in the *self-concept* conditions. The model is imprecise in specifying where the inflection point is when p is highly dependent on o. In the *accuracy* (low-dependence) conditions, the model predicts that attraction will rise monotonically as a function of the favorability of evaluation received. In the *ulterior motive* (high-dependence) conditions, the model predicts that attraction will rise to some point and will then decline as favorability of evaluation increases. Table 10 presents the mean attraction scores as depicted in Figure 5, except that subjects in the *self-concept* conditions have been further subdivided in terms of the mean evaluation received (in turn determined by their level of self-esteem). Within each level of context-defining instructions, subjects in the *self-concept* condition were divided into three subgroups of equal size, the remaining subject of the thirteen being allocated to that subgroup which would best equalize the within-subgroup ranges of evaluations received. In effect, the resulting values give us five rather than three points on the horizontal axis of the model diagram. It is interesting to note that this more detailed breakdown clearly

TABLE 10——— Evaluation received and rating scale attraction scores*

		POSITIVE	SELF-CONCEPT			NEUTRAL
	MEAN EVALUATION RECEIVED	96.00	124.40	135.75	163.75	192.00
ACCURACY	RANGE	96	117–128	131–143	155–177	192
	N	13	5	4	4	13
	MEAN ATTRACTION	22.54	23.00	26.25	29.25	40.31
ULTERIOR MOTIVE	MEAN EVALUATION RECEIVED	96.00	122.50	137.40	164.50	192.00
	RANGE	96	115–129	133–144	149–188	192
	N	13	4	5	4	13
	MEAN ATTRACTION	28.77	26.00	23.00	30.25	44.08

* Note—Lower evaluation scores indicate a more favorable evaluation. Lower attraction scores indicate greater attraction.

supports the attraction patterns predicted by the model: the attraction means in the *accuracy* conditions show a remarkably steady monotonic rise in response to increasingly positive feedback; the means in the *ulterior motive* conditions are, also without a single inversion, nonmonotonic and the inflection point occurs in the middle range of the evaluations received in the *self-concept* condition. If we restrict the analysis to those nine subjects in the *self-concept* conditions receiving a moderate evaluation, the interaction between instructions and high versus moderate evaluation received is significant in spite of the reduced N's. Such an analysis is, of course, post hoc. Nevertheless, the results of the analysis lend support to the original hypothesis and suggest that the model has some validity in the present situation.

A closer examination of the subjects' ratings on other dimensions and of their free descriptions of the observer in the *positive* and *self-concept* conditions, sheds an interesting light on their judgments. We have already reported the lack of any clear evidence that the subjects in the *ulterior motive* condition treated the positive evaluation received as an obvious gambit to curry favor. Under both instructional sets, subjects in the *positive* condition felt that the evaluations received were over-generous and in that sense flattering. However, it is clear that the positive evaluation conveyed somewhat different meanings to subjects in the two instructional conditions. For subjects in the *accuracy positive* condition, the favorable evaluation tended to be attributed to the observer's naivety, her congenital optimism, and her kindheartedness, but no manipulative intentions were cited. These subjects viewed the over-evaluation as a genuine reflection of something in the observer's personality structure, something which they obviously conceived of as a rather likable set of qualities. This affection for the *accuracy positive* observer developed in spite of the fact that the *accuracy self-concept* observer was judged to be brighter ($p < .01$) and more perceptive ($p < .001$) than the *accuracy positive* observer.

In contrast, the free descriptions of subjects in the flattery positive condition conveyed the implication that the observer was judged to be behaving out of weakness, insecurity, and fear of being rejected by the subjects. As objective evidence which bears on this impressionistic conclusion, subjects in the *ulterior motive positive* condition saw the observer as more maladjusted than subjects in the *ulterior motive self-concept* condition; on the other hand, subjects in the *accuracy positive* condition saw the observer as better adjusted than subjects in the *accuracy self-concept* condition. As Table 11 shows, these maladjustment ratings results contribute to a significant interaction. It is not clear why instructions designed to promote suspicions of acquisitive

TABLE 11——Ratings of psychological adjustment[*]
(high scores reflect better adjustment)

		POSITIVE	SELF-CONCEPT
ACCURACY	$\overline{X}$	10.69	9.85
	SD	(1.70)	(1.77)
ULTERIOR MOTIVE	$\overline{X}$	9.69	11.08
	SD	(1.80)	(1.66)

Note—Interaction F ratio (df: 1.48) $= 5.42$; $p < .05$
[*] Combining the ratings on the following items: "I would say that she is unusually mature and well adjusted," "I would not be surprised if she had some important personal problems" (reverse scored).

ingratiation resulted in impressions which treated the overly positive complimenter as a protective ingratiator (see chapter three). Perhaps the subjects were aware of the possible manipulative significance of the observer's behavior, but stopped short of committing themselves to this interpretation on a questionnaire to be seen by the experimenter.

Putting together the quantitative rating scale data and the qualitative free impressions, it is possible to draw the following picture of the impressions of the observer in the positive conditions. The observer in the *accuracy positive* condition was seen as rather weak and passive, not too bright, fairly secure and optimistic, and very likable and desirable as a friend. The observer in the *ulterior motive positive* condition was seen as defensive, fearful of creating a scene, not too bright, and generally insecure. She was not particularly well liked. As one would expect, the stage-setting instructions made much less difference in the self-concept conditions. Regardless of the context of feedback, subjects in the *self-concept* condition saw the observer as very intelligent, extremely perceptive, quite self-reliant, and even somewhat over-powering. More than a few subjects in this condition became quite uneasy, and described the experience as eerie and unsettling. Impressions of the observer in the neutral conditions were uniformly negative in tone, though the observer was usually given credit for her honesty and candor.

One of the most interesting findings of the Dickoff study was the absence of any relationship between the subject's attraction for the observer and the favorability of her own self-concept. In chapter two we reviewed briefly the results of an experiment by Deutsch and Solomon (1959) which was designed to test the hypothesis that we like those who like us only if we like ourselves. They found some support for this hypothesis in a setting where succeeding or failing subjects received approving or disapproving notes from a team member. In addition to the general effect that those sending approving notes were liked more than those sending disapproving notes, the subject was more positive toward the approving note sender if she had been successful and more positive toward the disapproving note sender if she had failed. Deutsch and Solomon's hypothesis, which is derived from Heider's (1958) balance theory, would lead us to predict that subjects high in self-esteem should respond with greater attraction to highly favorable evaluations than subjects with low self-esteem. The opposite should be true when the feedback is negative. As it turned out in Dickoff's experiment, the level of the subject's attraction for the observer was almost entirely a function of the favorability of the observer's evaluation, and bore no relation to her initial self-esteem in the *positive* and *neutral* conditions.

In attempting to understand why Deutsch and Solomon found evidence for the balance effect in the reciprocation of affection and Dickoff did not, two factors merit special consideration. In the first place, there were a number of important differences between the two studies which might have a direct bearing on the impact of the evaluation received. In the Deutsch and Solomon study, self-evaluations were manipulated by the experimenter and pertained to restricted areas of performance which were probably not centrally involved in the average subject's self-picture. In Dickoff's study the observer's judgments were of many complex and important aspects of the self. Furthermore, the feedback was sustained and occurred in the context of a highly involving task of anticipation learning. There was plenty of time for the breadth and the level of the evaluation to sink in. In a later study Deutsch (1960) asked groups of subjects to imagine how they would have reacted in the performance evaluation situation of the Deutsch and Solomon experiment. These bystanders did not show any evidence of the balance effect seen in the original experiment, but tended to like the approving note sender and to dislike the disapproving one, regardless of their own imagined experience of success or failure. Deutsch himself suggests that the bystanders did not react like the original "involved" subjects because they over-estimated the decisiveness of the evaluation contained in the note. It might be suggested, then, that the more decisive and all-encompassing the positive or negative evaluation received, the less the tendency for any balance effect to show itself, and the greater the tendency for attraction to correlate with level of received evaluation.

Another point of comparison involves the factor of credibility. In Dickoff's study there is evidence of a general balance effect in the *ulterior motive* conditions. Both the model and the Dickoff results agree that when perceived dependence is high, the person will be less attracted to those who are extremely favorable than to those who are reasonably favorable. If there is no reason to doubt the accuracy of the evaluation received, however, the relation between attraction given and evaluation received is monotonic throughout the range of positive evaluation studied. It is conceivable that some of the subjects who received approving notes after failure in the Deutsch and Solomon experiment were suspicious about the origins of the note, assumed that a mistake was made in transmission, or at least were led to question the credibility of the source.

While additional research should certainly be addressed to this issue, it is our present feeling that balance effects will most likely manifest themselves under two conditions: when an overly positive evaluation raises suspicions about the source's motives and when there is ample evidence on other grounds that the evaluator likes, respects, or admires the subject. With respect to the latter point, without exception the studies reported in the present monograph deal with first-impression situations in which the information exchanged between two people defines their respective evaluations of one another. At later stages of the acquaintance process, it very well may be that a judge's conception of his own positive and negative attributes plays a more important role in his favorability judgments of others. If our previous interactions with another person have convinced us that he is basically attracted to us, we may be more attracted to him when he agrees with us about both positive and negative characteristics than when he dispenses uniform praise. Newcomb (1956) presented some suggestive evidence showing that mutual friends in a college dormitory attributed both negative and positive qualities to each other in a pattern which agreed closely with the self-ratings of the recipient. (In a latter and more comprehensive account of data from these and other subjects, however, no explicit reference is made to the problem; cf. Newcomb, 1961.) While we are woefully lacking in data on the relations between evaluations received and attraction granted at later stages of the acquaintance process, it seems reasonable to suggest that firm and trusted friends can openly recognize and sympathize with our weaknesses without damaging the friendly relationship. In the first impression situation studied by Dickoff, however, general liking and attraction is geared to the positiveness of a received evaluation—no matter how extreme—and only perceptions of intelligence and social perceptiveness show a decline as the evaluation received becomes more positive than the self-concept. We may admire and pay tribute to one who correctly differentiates our strengths and weaknesses in a first-impression setting, but Dickoff's data suggest that we do not necessarily like or feel comfortable with such a person.

THE EVALUATION OF A CONFORMIST

The results of Dickoff's study generally supported the model linking the independent variables of "degree of tactical use" and perceived dependence to the dependent variable of attraction. The tactic involved was the direct receipt of compliments by a target person from a potential ingratiator, and perceived dependence was coordinated to the possibility that attraction could be sought in the service of reaping personal advantage. Our next task is to see whether the model also holds in the area of conformity behavior. Unfortunately, however, a special methodological problem intervenes in the attempt to design an experimental test of the model with the tactic of conformity as the medium of potential ingratiation. A straightforward way to test the model would seem to require a situation in which a subject (o) presents his opinions to another person (p) who uniformly agrees with the opinions expressed or is generally supportive but variable in his degree of agreement. This opinion "exchange" could occur in a setting in which p was either high or low in dependence on o. The difficulty with this arrangement is that there is no way, short of selecting os who all have identical opinions, to hold constant the pattern of opinions actually endorsed by p while varying the degree of agreement between p and o. Let us assume that o, who always expresses his opinions first, endorses a particular pattern of beliefs on a variety of issues. Quite independently of his own beliefs, he might have a different impression of a responding p who expressed the same pattern and one who expressed a second pattern. It is quite likely that such a difference in impression would have measurable effects on any index of subsequent attraction or evaluation. Presumably, o would like someone who endorsed the first pattern better than someone who endorsed the second pattern, both because the first pattern involves agreement with his own views and because the second pattern will be judged to provide evidence that p is inconsistent, fuzzy-minded, biased, or uninformed.

If it could somehow be arranged that p always expressed the same pattern of opinions in each condition, but ended up in close versus variable agreement with *o*, then differences in *o*'s impression of *p* would have to be a function of the degree of perceived agreement and not of the judged validity of the opinions expressed. An experiment by Jones, Jones, and Gergen (1963) attempted to accomplish this objective by the simple expedient of having subjects observe an interaction between two others rather than participate in the interaction as the opinion-initiating target person. In this study, referred to previously as the Mike and Paul experiment because of the fictitious names assigned to the actors, 150 male undergraduate subjects listened to tape-recorded opinion interchanges between two students, one of whom always expressed his opinions second. In some cases these opinions agreed closely with the opinions of the first student (*close* treatment); in other cases they were still in general agreement but showed more variation (*variable* treatment). In other words, one independent variable was the consistency and extremity of tactical use (paraphrasing the label of the abscissa in Figure 4). In keeping with the desire to avoid the problem of confounding discussed above, it should be emphasized that the second student always expressed exactly the same opinions and his behavior was thus identical from cell to cell of the design. Variations in agreement were arranged by having the *first* student state different opinions in the *same* and *variable* conditions.

Cross-cutting the close-variable manipulation was an instructional variable designed to vary the extent to which the second student was perceived to be dependent on the first student in the taped interchange. In each experimental session, the experimenter introduced the study as one dealing with impression formation. The subjects were told that they would listen to a tape recording of a discussion between two undergraduate volunteers which had occurred during the preceding year. They were specifically instructed to pay attention to everything which would be said by the volunteer B, in this case the person in a position to conform. A copy of the opinion items to be used was distributed to the subjects in order to aid them in following the recording more closely. The experimenter then turned on the tape recording.

The moderator on the tape recording introduced the experimental situation to the two volunteers (both actually role players following a carefully prepared script) in one of two ways. Approximately half of the subjects in the experimental conditions heard the moderator describe the purpose of the taped interaction to the role players as a preliminary procedure for selecting highly compatible pairs to participate in a subsequent problem-solving experiment. It was made clear that compatibility would be determined by the role players' evaluations of each other after the exchange of opinions. The problem-solving experiment was described not only as very interesting and worthwhile, but the volunteers were further told that if they turned out to be compatible they could earn $2.50 an hour in future sessions. Both role players responded with considerable enthusiasm to the prospect of qualifying for the subsequent sessions. This combination of instructions and role player response constituted the *high-dependence* condition, since B was presumably dependent on A for attaining the desirable goal of participation in the subsequent experiment.

The other half of the subjects heard the experiment described to the volunteers as one concerned with impression formation. They were merely to indicate their degree of agreement or disagreement with a number of opinion statements, and in the process, try to formulate a clear impression of each other (*low-dependence* condition).

Results.   The main predictions of the Jones, Jones, and Gergen (1963) study concern a bystander's evaluations of a person in a position to conform to someone else. These predictions logically require, however, that the subjects draw certain inferences about social influence effects as a joint function of the discussion context and the relationship between the two sets of expressed opinions. Specifically, subjects exposed to the high-dependence close condition, relative to those in other conditions, should perceive B to be lacking in independence and candor in making his responses to A.

As Table 12 shows, conformity is inferred as a matter of course when one person closely agrees with another on a rather large collection of opinion items. Such a person is seen as easily

TABLE 12—— Ratings of conformity, candor, and self-promotion (means, standard deviations, and significant treatment effects)

			ITEM CLUSTER*			
			CONFORMITY	CANDOR	SELF-PROMOTION	N
HIGH-DEP.	C	$\overline{X}$	20.23	10.79	13.41	22
		SD	3.03	3.93	2.74	
	V	$\overline{X}$	14.52	16.57	10.14	21
		SD	4.20	2.34	2.90	
LOW-DEP.	C	$\overline{X}$	19.39	12.97	10.68	31
		SD	3.57	3.83	3.10	
	V	$\overline{X}$	16.67	14.76	11.43	21
		SD	4.00	3.48	2.80	
SIGNIFICANT†		C-V	$p < .001$	$p < .001$	$p < .05$	
EFFECTS		H-L	—	—	—	95
		INTERACTION	—	$p < .01$	$p < .01$	

* Higher mean scores signify more of the attribute labeled in each column.

† Because of unequal cell frequencies, these effects were tested by the approximation technique using group means as entries.

influenced and lacking in independence. Inferences concerning the intent underlying this conformity behavior, however, are more clearly a function of the degree to which the conformist is perceived to be dependent on the target of conformity. The combination of high-dependence and marked opinion agreement clearly leads to the inference that B's conformity reflects a lack of candor.

There is additional evidence in the data on perceived self-promotion to support the conclusion that the dependence variable affected subjects' inferences about the intentions underlying conformity. In the low-dependence conditions close B is seen as more cooperative and less "self-promotive" than variable B. Under high-dependence instructions, on the other hand, close B is seen as *less* cooperative than variable B. The interaction involving these comparisons is significant ($p < .01$). Such a pattern of findings logically paves the way for a test of the hypotheses concerning more general aspects of evaluation.

The main experimental hypothesis proposed that B would be more negatively evaluated for closely agreeing with A when his dependence on A was high than when it was low. In order to test this proposition, the subject's ratings of B on four traits directly reflecting likability and desirability as a friend were subjected to a two (high-low dependence) by two (close-variable discrepancy) analysis of variance. The results were a significant main effect for discrepancy (B was better liked when his agreement was variable than when it was close) and, as predicted, a significant interaction between dependence and discrepancy ($F = 7.705$, $p < .01$). As Figure 6 shows, the significant interaction reflects an unexpected contribution from the high-attractiveness ratings given to B when he is highly dependent but variable in his agreement. Thus, relative to the *low-dependence* B, not only is the *high-dependence* B seen as less attractive when he agrees closely with A ($p < .05$); he is seen as *more* attractive when he is variable in his agreement ($p < .10$). This latter trend may reflect the subject's appreciation *as a bystander* of B's integrity in the face of pressures to dissimulate. The person who is the target of variable agreement under high-dependence conditions might not show the same positive attitudes toward B. The model predicts that he would not.

Since B in all cases endorsed the same opinion ratings, it is clear that these variations in his perceived attractiveness were a function of the two independent variables and their combined effect on attributions of manipulative intent. In coming to terms with the results, it is important to realize that both the *close* and the *variable* B's were generally in agreement with A on every

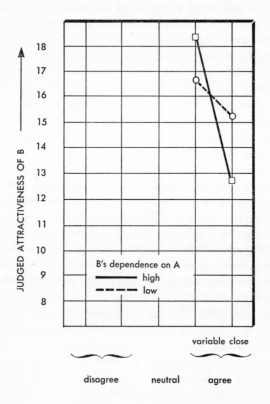

FIGURE 6——Personal attractiveness ratings as a function of experimental conditions

opinion issue. In no case did B actually take an opposing stand, or differ from A by more than six of the twelve rating points. The difference in discrepancy was merely a difference in the extent and the monotonous regularity of agreement. From one point of view, we may regard the discrepancy dimension as a dimension of subtlety in the use of ingratiation—thus we might have labeled the horizontal axis in Figure 4 "obviousness" of tactical use. At least from a bystander's perspective, the greater the importance of A liking B, the more it behooves B to show less than complete agreement with A's opinions. In more general terms, this is precisely what is indicated by the model depicted in Figure 4.

The model has shown some success in predicting the pattern of attraction in response both to other-enhancement and conformity tactics. There is no experimental evidence as yet that the model applies to tactics other than compliments received and agreement with one's opinion, though it seems plausible that it would. In the general area of self-presentation, for example, describing oneself with great and uniform immodesty should be especially unrewarding in conditions of high dependence (for example, during a job interview, or on an application for admission to graduate school). Excessive favors or elaborate gifts should also lead to negative feelings and tend to boomerang when the giver can potentially receive more from the recipient than he can bestow.

The Bystander and the Target Person

An interesting set of issues center around the possible differential reactions of target persons and bystanders to the same potentially ingratiating actor. Reverting to our simple notational system, assume that p gives o a positive x in the presence of q (a bystander), x being a series of compliments, agreements, vigorous head nods. There are a number of reasons why one would predict that q would be quicker to infer manipulative intent than o. In the case of other-enhancement, whereas o has a strong, vain desire to assign credibility to compliments sent his way, q's own vanity should not be engaged and the discrepancy between o's apparent attributes and those assigned to him by p should be more evident to q. (It may also be the case that q is in competition with p for o's favor, making his threshold for perceiving p's flattery even lower.) In the case of conformity, it is important to inquire whether o and q share the same opinions. If they do not, then obviously o should be more favorably disposed to a conforming p simply because the two are in closer opinion agreement than are q and p. As far as other tactical forms are concerned, any behavior designed specifically to please o and tailor-made for o's individual preferences would, on the average, elicit a more favorable response from o than from bystander q. In addition to the factors of vanity and similarity mentioned above, there is the pervasive difference that o is engaged in responding to p whereas q is by definition a passive observer. Not only should the pressure to respond create a kind of urgency in o which does not favor discernment and incisive social perception, but o is likely to respond overtly to p with a courtesy and warmth which may also characterize his more private attitudes.

The empirical evidence on bystander-target person differences is slim but suggestive. In the Jones, Jones, and Gergen (1963) study just described, subjects were asked to record both their own feelings and to predict how the target person (the recipient of conformity) would respond. The results show that the suspected conformist is evaluated more negatively when the subjects are expressing their own evaluations as bystanders than when they are attempting to predict the evaluation which would be made by the target person. Since there was no evidence that the subjects thought A was particularly gullible, stupid, or in need of support, we believe that the finding itself has general significance and could be replicated with different persons playing the roles of A and B. However, it remains to be determined whether the subjects attempting to predict A's evaluation of B are simply misjudging the potency of the situation from A's point of view (manifesting the kind of "pathetic fallacy" described by Deutsch, 1960), *or* whether the predictions reflect an accurate intuition that the target of an ingratiation attempt is more likely to be taken in by it.

Either of these alternatives, if true, would have interesting implications for the psychology of ingratiation and its perception. In order to choose between them, it is obviously necessary to determine how targets of conformity actually do respond to a conformist. Because of the complicated technical problems of experimental control involved in such a study, we chose the present bystander version. The main problem is to find a way to vary closeness of B's agreement without also varying the pattern of attitudes endorsed by B. Nevertheless, the theoretical issues seem of sufficient interest and importance to call for investigation along lines similar to the present study, but in which a naive initiator is questioned about his evaluations of a closely agreeing experimental confederate.

SUMMARY AND CONCLUSIONS

In this chapter we have shifted our focus from the perspective of the ingratiator to that of the target person and have endorsed the reasoning that the latter perspective is the obverse of the former and therefore no new principles are involved in accounting for the target person's reactions. However, it was also argued that the target person is apt to cover up his true feelings about the ingratiator and conceal from him any suspicions of the ingratiator's intentions. To the extent that this is true, the ingratiator receives very poor, nondiscriminating feedback to guide his tactical behavior. Also, the target person may find it difficult to maintain negative attitudes toward the ingratiator in private while behaving positively toward him.

The major portion of the chapter was devoted to a model relating the degree, intensity, or obviousness of tactical behavior to the level of social dependence in predicting the target person's attraction ratings. The main feature of interest in the model is the fate of someone who behaves in an extremely ingratiating manner toward a person upon whom he is dependent. The results of Dickoff's (1961) study gave qualified support to the model in showing that the recipients of lavish praise from another are more positively attracted to him when he is not dependent on them for help or benefit. This difference in the attractiveness of dependent and nondependent complimenters occurs in spite of the absence of any evidence that ulterior motives are attributed to the dependent complimenter. Instead the dependent complimenter is seen as insecure and maladjusted. This rather curious substitute for attributions of manipulative intent may reflect the subjects' desire to justify their negative feelings (to themselves and the experimenter) without committing themselves to the more drastic accusation of acquisitive ingratiation. Another interesting finding in the Dickoff (1961) study was the absence of any relationship between self-esteem and responses to overly positive or overly negative evaluations from another. As long as the evaluation received is credible, the more positive it is the more attracted the target person becomes to the evaluator.

The results of a second study by Jones, Jones, and Gergen (1963) again supported the model, this time with respect to the tactic of conformity. The subjects were bystanders listening to an opinion exchange, rather than target persons as in the Dickoff study. They were more attracted to the potential ingratiator when he was variable in his agreement than when he was slavishly close, and this was especially true when the opinion exchange took place in a context wherein the ingratiator was dependent on the target person for his approval. While the significant interaction between opinion discrepancy and dependence was in line with the model, the model did not predict more attraction for the high-dependent variable conformer than for the low-dependent variable conformer. It may be that the favorable attitude toward the high-dependent variable conformer was a special function of the subject's position as a bystander and that the model accurately predicts a target person's response to conformity variations. This is an interesting conjecture to be pursued in future research.

The problem of mapping the conditions affecting one's judgments of a potential ingratiator is a manageable one, but the experiments presented here obviously do little more than scratch the surface. Futher research within the paradigm suggested by our model is eminently worth pursuing not only because of the insights into the subtleties of ingratiation that might accrue, but also because of the light that might be shed on the general problem of motive attribution in the process of interpersonal perception.

7 Conclusions and Prospects

In the experiments reported in this monograph we have sought to introduce the ulterior motive of attraction-seeking into the early stages of the acquaintance process and have tried to identify its behavioral consequences. Our basic position has been that the tactical considerations involved in managing a positive impression weave through the fabric of normal interpersonal action and shape those communications which have implications for gaining and maintaining esteem. The experimental strategy employed in the preceding studies has taken advantage of the fact that tactical considerations are more salient in certain contexts than others, and has followed from the conviction that these contexts can be arranged by experimental staging. We are convinced, however, that settings in which tactical considerations are prominent are neither rare nor socially trivial. By our focus on the changes in behavior occasioned by increasing the importance of winning attraction, we hope that we have raised questions germane to a more general analysis of social interaction and self-presentation.

In this closing chapter, it is appropriate to review and recapitulate the major themes of our research and to extract from such a review suggestions for future empirical investigation. While the emphasis will be on new lines of inquiry, we are well aware that much additional effort could be fruitfully expended in verifying and replicating the relationships which have been reported in the preceding chapters.

There seems little room for doubt that the average undergraduate subject behaves differently in a setting in which he wants to be liked than in a setting in which he is striving to be an accurate informant about himself. When conditions are so arranged that creating a positive impression is emphasized, subjects utilize certain mechanisms of accommodating to the target person which apparently have been used to cope with settings arousing similar concerns outside the laboratory. In each experiment in the current series, the experimenter poses a complicated interpersonal problem for the subject and drastically restricts his resources for coping with the problem. The subject exposed to ingratiation instructions is to impress another person with words, or multiple-choice selections, or rating-scale checks, and thereby secure affection for himself as a person. The possibilities of respectful and sympathetic attention, of casual explorations of similar interests, or of the discovery of mutual friends are not available. In some cases, the subject faces the additional handicap implied by the target person's knowledge of the subject's dependent position—his stake in a positive evaluation. In all cases, the subject's behavior is being monitored by the experimenter who posed the problem in the first place, but who shows no disposition to provide specific suggestions as to how it should be solved.

In the face of these restrictions and ambiguities, the average subject—whether male or female—becomes involved in a strategic problem-solving performance; and enough subjects choose the same solution to lead to significant regularities in the resulting patterns of ingratiation. In the terms of the major dependent variable categories introduced in chapter two, let us examine some of the principal empirical regularities obtained along with the factors which qualify their generality. In each case, the reactions of subjects in an ingratiation condition are implicitly contrasted with the reactions of subjects in a control situation—that is, one designed to minimize the concern of creating an attractive impression.

Self-presentation.   If subjects are instructed to describe themselves in such a way as to make a good impression, the general tendency is for them to emphasize their positive attributes and to play down their weaknesses in the self-description task. However, a number of variables have been shown to affect this tendency. In specifying these variables we move closer to a more useful theoretical statement of the conditions underlying self-enhancement. One such variable is the ingratiator's relative position in an hierarchical organization. In the experiment with ROTC students, low-status subjects became more self-enhancing only on those attributes they considered unimportant. High-status subjects actually became more modest. Since the superiority of the high-status students was quite secure and buttressed by differences in age and seniority, we might suggest that they were sufficiently impressive by dint of their social position alone and could afford to use the self-description scale to increase their approachability or their openness to friendly overtures. If their position had been less secure, the high-status subjects might have shown a greater disposition to advertise their strengths in important, status-related areas.

The business game experiment showed that the characteristics of the target person have an influence on the particular attributes emphasized in self-description (though this influence occurs even in the control condition) and that persons attempting to bias a supervisor in their favor tend to do so by describing themselves as competent and respectworthy rather than friendly and affable. This experiment raises the question of what is meant by seeking attraction, and makes it clear that different components of attractiveness are likely to be involved in different ingratiation settings. When the goal is to win a positive rating for task performance different strengths will be stressed than when the goal is to be judged a congenial or compatible partner (as in the ROTC study).

Finally, it seems likely that the variable of mutual versus asymmetrical awareness is important. In several experiments the subject and the target person were both equally aware, presumably, of the subject's dependence. In others, the subject was privately instructed to create a positive impression and was assured that the target person was unaware of these instructions. In the latter cases the tendency toward self-enhancement was strong and tended to pervade all personal characteristics equally. When the subject realized that the target person was aware of his stake in creating a positive impression, however, there was more of a tendency to be self-enhancing in one area and self-deprecating in another. The fact that the target person is aware of the subject's dependence seems to call forth more subtle and complicated tactical variations, variations designed to establish the subject's credentials as a trustworthy communicator at the same time as they highlight his virtues in important areas. The areas considered important are in turn determined by the structure of the experimental setting, and the sorts of variables described in the preceding paragraphs.

Conformity.   One of the clearest and most reliable findings of. the present monograph is that instructions to promote ingratiation result in movements toward greater public agreement with the target person's stated opinions. This general effect is found among high- and low-status subjects alike, and appears to be a readily aroused component of ingratiation strategy. Again, however, the results of different experiments point to qualifying conditions having interesting theoretical implications. While both high- and low-status subjects conformed more under ingratiation than under control instructions, the pattern of conformity was affected by the relevance of item content to the basis of the hierarchy. Low-status subjects conformed more on relevant than on irrelevant items and high-status subjects conformed more on irrelevant than relevant items.

A second qualification emerged from the business game study results. Strategic or effect-oriented conformity may be inhibited or promoted by variations in the personal values of the target person, insofar as these values relate to the conformer's subjective probability of winning favor through agreement. In other words, if the target person clearly values tact, cooperation, and getting along with others, he is likely to be vulnerable to the strategic use of opinion agreement. The business game experiment showed that subjects were quick to read this conclusion and to take advantage of this perceived vulnerability.

Finally, ingratiation instructions have a greater effect when initial opinion discrepancy is high than when the ingratiator and the target person start out in fairly close agreement. Part of this difference is undoubtedly attributable to the lack of room for movement in the close agreement case, but there is some evidence supporting the notion that too much agreement is avoided for reasons of strategic effect.

The fact that undergraduates can be so easily induced to modify their opinions in order to win attraction has important social implications, as others have noted, but it should be recognized that "movement toward" does not mean "agreement with." In the experimental conditions in which significant conformity occurred most often, this conformity has a compromise between the subject's initial opinion and the discrepant opinion of the target person. Thus the ingratiator shows some accommodation to the highly divergent opinion of the target person, but he avoids having to face any blatant evidence of his own conformity and he avoids arousing suspicions in the target person that his agreement is perhaps too close to be coincidental. He might be described as avoiding extreme disagreement rather than seeking close agreement, but the evidence that his expressed opinions are influenced by his desire to create an attractive impression is clear.

Other-enhancement.   The evidence concerning other-enhancement in response to ingratiation instructions is quite inconclusive. Only two studies dealt with other-enhancement as a dependent variable, and in both of these the opportunity to rate the target person was last in the chain of experimental tasks with which the subject was burdened. In one of these studies, low-status subjects were more inclined to be complimentary in their ratings of high-status partners after ingratiation instructions than in the control condition; the variation in conditions did not affect the high-status raters. This difference was unexpected and remains difficult to account for, although there is some evidence that compliments from low- to high-status persons in a hierarchy result in a boomerang in the form of attraction decline: the high-status subjects felt that the low-status subjects were quite flattering and insincere in the ingratiation versus the control condition.

The information conveyed by the low- to the high-status subjects was identical in the two conditions.

In the other study in which an opportunity for other-enhancement was provided, no differences were obtained. A more direct experimental attack on the use of compliments is clearly needed before any conclusions are warranted concerning the conditions affecting their use. It is very important that such studies be conducted with appropriate control comparisons, since target persons who have the power to benefit are quite likely to receive positive ratings—because they are in fact impressive, have achieved success, and so on—independently of the dependent person's intent to be ingratiating. Designs comparing private and public ratings might be feasible, except for the problem of the subject's tendency to commit himself to whichever rating came first. In other words, one rating would be likely to affect the other unless they were well disguised parallel forms. It may turn out that compliments, more than conformity or self-presentation, require a context of interaction less rigid and constraining than the settings created in our experiments.

Perceptions of those in a dependent position.   In the preceding chapter, we presented a simple model for predicting differences in the evaluation of a potential ingratiator as a function of the dependence context in which his behavior takes place. With increasing dependence on the target person, increasing subtlety is required on the part of the would-be ingratiator. We have just reviewed the result showing that high-status subjects attributed greater insincerity to low-status subjects in the ingratiation than in the control condition, in spite of the fact that their behavior was identical (and uniformly positive) in the two settings. Two other experiments, reviewed in the preceding chapter, gave general support to the shape of the model and showed its applicability to opinion agreement and other-enhancement. There was some evidence in the opinion agreement study that a person is especially liked if he is placed under pressure to conform and avoids the appearance of uniform or slavish agreement. We do not know as yet whether this result occurred because our subjects were bystanders rather than target persons, or whether other special features of the experiment might have produced the result. But it is likely that there are effective mixtures of agreement and disagreement which enhance a person's attractiveness to a high degree. Such mixtures are more likely to gain favor in high-dependence contexts than is uniform agreement.

DIRECTIONS FOR FURTHER RESEARCH

The experiments reported in this monograph have involved procedural variations on a common methodological theme—comparing situations in which attraction is salient with those in which it is not. The conceptual variable, high versus low dependence, has been operationalized in different ways from experiment to experiment, and we see both advantages and disadvantages in such a strategy. The advantages are those associated with freeing interpretation from its ties with particular operations and allowing us to talk with greater confidence about dependence as a theoretical construct. When the results of two or more experiments dovetail in a sensible way, we are ahead of the game for having chosen theoretically equivalent but operationally different independent variables. The disadvantages are that precise replication is foregone, and we do not know whether failures of prediction in a particular experiment would have been avoided if slightly different instructions had been employed in the manipulation. Such disadvantages are compounded by other changes from study to study: the tendency to use similar but not identical dependent variable measures, sex of experimental subjects, context of recruitment, and identity of experimenter.

It should thus be clear that our use of the laboratory experiment cannot at present be justified as part of a strategy of cumulative theoretical confirmation. The experimental method was chosen as much to raise and define, as to solve, our interpretive problems. Hopefully, then, we should now be in a better position to see what these problems are and to adopt more focused strategies toward their solution.

The first problem which comes to mind concerns the role of self-deception and retrospective distortion in the launching and justification of tactical behavior. We have not considered, in this monograph, the extreme case in which one person deliberately contrives to best another in a self-conscious, calculated manner. While for purposes of easier communication we have spoken of the ingratiator's "design" or "intent" and his "decision" to ingratiate, our post-experimental questionnaire data typically revealed no clear awareness of strategies adopted or even, very often, of an interest in gaining attraction. In some cases our instructions openly encouraged dissimulation, but we in no case relieved the subject entirely of his responsibility for choosing the particular mode of self-presentation which would be compatible with his own standards. Chapter three explored some of the ways in which subjects managed to maintain face in the process of ingratiation. Several of these ways involved distortions of contextual cues and of the representativeness or self-relevant quality of their own behavior. This is an intriguing domain for further investigation, especially since there is at least some available theory to guide hypothesis formulation. Of special interest is the effect that indulging in the tactics of ingratiation has on the ingratiator's subsequent behavior, his conception of himself, and his attitudes toward the target person. Dissonance theory alerts us to the importance of choice and commitment in the assimilation of one's private attitudes with one's public behavior. The theory would suggest that the more compelling the justification for ingratiating behavior, the less this behavior will affect subsequent attitudes toward the self, and the less some ingratiation will lead to more ingratiation. Such reasoning opens new lines of investigation into the effects of varying the number or strength of forces inducing the subject to be ingratiating. We might start with the general proposition that ingratiation tactics induced by minimally sufficient conditions should lead to greater cognitive work, greater retrospective distortion, in the service of dissonance reduction. But such conditions as the incentive value of attraction, the subjective probability of success, and the perceived legitimacy of tactical overtures, may not be additive and may be differentially sensitive to dissonance reduction efforts. Will the ingratiator, under conditions of minimal induction, push toward an overvaluation of the target person and exaggerate the importance of the latter's approval? Will he engage in private self-enhancement to assure himself that he deserves the benefits sought? Will he develop a new and more complex ethic to justify his dissimulation? What are the contextual social conditions which determine the particular cognitive work which is likely to take place?

A second route for building upon the data we now have would carry us into further research on the psychology of power differences and their vicissitudes. Since the results of the completed experiments leave us in a better position to identify ingratiating overtures, it is possible to push into contexts and introduce arousal conditions which are more remote from mere instructions to create a positive impression. The business game experiment, especially, opens up new and intriguing areas of investigation. In that study, subjects interested in influencing the supervisor tried to do so by impressing him with their competence rather than their affable eagerness to reciprocate affection. If the supervisor's power were more general and ubiquitous in its potential implications for the subject's welfare, would he be more inclined to go after the supervisor's friendship in addition to his respect? Are there likely to be differences in tactics employed as a function of the expected duration of the relationship? If a relationship containing persons of different power or status is likely to be circumscribed and of short duration, the low-status person may be more reckless in his choice of ingratiation tactics and avoid the subtleties which more durable relations would seem to require. The more permanent the relationship is likely to be, the more opportunities the ingratiator has to arrange appropriate contexts for applying his art, and the greater his stake in avoiding a boomerang effect.

A third area, the difficulties and opportunities of which are highlighted by the present research, is that in which the study of person perception intersects with the study of self-presentation. As we have repeatedly argued, social interaction inevitably involves more than an exchange of information about external objects and events. The actors are concurrently exchanging information *about each other*, information which qualifies, validates, or vitiates the surface meaning of what is being said about the larger environment. Our knowledge about another person helps us to interpret his behavior, but this knowledge is also being continually modified by this behavior. Nor does the cognitive complexity underlying social interaction stop here, for our impression of another conditions the way in which we present ourself to him which in turn affects his behavior in rejoinder. The considerations involved here transcend the study of ingratiation, but the linkage between the dynamics of self-presentation and social perception is never firmer than when positive, potentially ingratiating, overtures are involved. We have commented on the special ambiguity of compliments and conformity, and this is an ambiguity which the recipient must resolve in order to decide whether to approach or avoid the ingratiator, whether to accept his warm appraisal as sincere and his opinions as independently derived. Further investigation into the resolution process may shed considerable light on the dynamics of phenomenal causality, or the attribution of intentions. A specific line of further inquiry would tie the study of ingratiation more closely to studies of communicator credibility in attitude-change research: confronted with the limited resources of more or less agreement or with appraisals which are more or less complimentary, how does the communicator establish his credentials of sincerity without offending the other by his disagreements or his criticisms? Under what circumstances is credibility irrelevant—that is, under what conditions is obvious flattery attributable to benign motivation, and under what conditions is the flatterer excused because of the very fact that his great stake in gaining approval is understood?

None of the present experiments has dealt with the matter of favors and services in the general framework of self-presentation. There are fascinating complexities here that are worthy of exploration. Under what conditions is a favor expected and accepted as a matter of course? When does a favor succeed in making the giver more attractive to the beneficiary? When do favors produce negative and avoidance reactions? Turning the argument around, is it possible that others like us more when we let them do small favors *for us?* If this could be demonstrated (and it has been suggested as a powerful strategic principle by Webb and Morgan, 1930), what would be the psychological dynamic behind the effectiveness of such a tactic?

To inquire into questions of the empirical generality of specific experimental results is to open a Pandora's box of investigative possibilities. The question of individual differences in "ingratiation thresholds" has been touched upon at various points, but it certainly has not been emphasized in the design or analysis of the experiments reported. It would probably be both profitable and intriguing to explore the family backgrounds and personality traits of subjects with low versus high thresholds of ingratiation. The related question of subcultural variation in the forms of, and occasions for, manipulative behavior would add an interesting dimension to our study and to broader issues of cross-cultural variation. Every society and subgroup must develop norms which govern the balance of accuracy and social accommodation in interpersonal communications. To uncover the various cultural modes for handling this problem would provide a new and useful wedge into the study of behavioral reflections of cultural prescriptions and into the special problem of taking advantage of the adherence of others to norms.

Conclusions

The present monograph has tried to grapple with the complexities of a sprawling and rather amorphous domain of interpersonal behavior: that which is in some sense strategically oriented toward the elicitation or maintenance of attraction. A peculiarity of the attempted analysis has been that, in a way, the microscopic scrutiny of ingratiation reveals an evanescent phenomenon which in any given case turns into something equally well identified by some other name. We find ourselves dealing with the conditions of social conformity, or the norms of status deference, or the determinants of communicator credibility, or the conditions of exploitative bargaining. Are there any real advantages to the use of such a semi-popular concept of ingratiation when we end up talking about a vaguely bounded cluster of social influence strategies each having its own phenotypic properties? One of the major advantages seems to be the research stimulus value of relating a socially important topic like ingratiation, or flattery, to more basic processes of motivation, perception, and affective communication. A related advantage is that by showing how social perception, attitude-change, and self-presentation strategies are related to ingratiation, we shed some light on how they are related to each other. Conformity takes on new aspects when viewed not only as a product of, but also a strategy in the service of, social influence. The emerging field of self-presentation takes on structure when we see its relations with person perception and the risks of unbridled attraction-seeking. A further advantage is that the study of ingratiation confronts us dramatically with the social interaction episode, and the overlapping but always differing perspectives of the actors involved. The present effort is only a beginning foray in the direction of understanding more clearly what is involved in one important cluster of social responses, but perhaps it at least has the merit of placing old issues in a new light and bringing a phenomenon with a lively history in literary discourse into the domain of systematic psychological inquiry.

References

ADAMS, J. S. Toward an understanding of inequity. *J. abnorm. soc. Psychol.*, 1963, *67*, 422–437.

ARONSON, E. The effect of effort on the attractiveness of rewarded and unrewarded stimuli. *J. abnorm. soc. Psychol.*, 1961, *63*, 375–381.

ARONSON, E. & CARLSMITH, J. M. The effect of severity of threat on the devaluation of forbidden behavior. *J. abnorm. soc. Psychol.*, 1963, *66*, 584–589.

ATKINSON, J. W. Motivational determinants of risk-taking behavior. *Psychol. Rev.*, 1957, *64*, 359–373.

BALES, R. F. Task roles and social roles in problem-solving groups. In Eleanor Maccoby, T. Newcomb, E. L. Hartley (Eds.), *Readings in social psychology*. (3rd ed.) New York: Holt, 1958.

BARTLETT, J. *Familiar Quotations*. Boston: Little, Brown, 1882.

BLAU, P. M. A theory of social integration. *Amer. J. Sociol.*, 1960, *65*, 545–557.

BLAU, P. M. *Exchange and Power in Social Life*. New York: Wiley, 1964.

BREHM, J. W. & COHEN, A. R. *Explorations in cognitive dissonance*. New York: Wiley, 1962.

CARNEGIE, D. *How to win friends and influence people*. New York: Simon and Schuster, 1936.

CHESTERFIELD, Earl of (Philip Darmer Stanhope) *Letters to his son* (Walter M. Dunne, Ed.) New York: Wiley, 1901. Original publ. 1774.

CHRISTIE, R. & MERTON, R. K. Procedures for the sociological study of the values climate of medical schools. *J. med. Educ.*, 1958, *33*, 125–153.

COHEN, A. R. Some implications of self-esteem for social influence. In C. I. Hovland & I. L. Janis (Eds.), *Personality and persuasibility*, New Haven: Yale, 1959.

COOLEY, C. H. *Human nature and the social order*. New York: Scribner, 1922.

DAVIS, K. E. & JONES, E. E. Changes in interpersonal perception as a means of reducing cognitive dissonance. *J. abnorm. soc. Psychol.*, 1960, *61*, 402–410.

deCHARMS, R. & ROSENBAUM, M. E. Status variables and matching behavior. *J. Pers.*, 1960, *28*, 492–502.

DEUTSCH, M. The pathetic fallacy: an observer error in social perception. *J. Pers.*, 1960, *28*, 317–332.

DEUTSCH, M. & GERARD, H. B. A study of normative and informational social influences upon individual judgment. *J. abnorm. soc. Psychol.*, 1955, *51*, 629–636.

DEUTSCH, M. & SOLOMON, L. Reactions to evaluations by others as influenced by self-evaluations. *Sociometry*, 1959, *22*, 93–112.

DICKOFF, Hilda. Reactions to evaluations by another person as a function of self-evaluation and the interaction context. Unpublished doctoral dissertation, Duke University, 1961.

ESCALONA, S. K. The effect of success and failure upon the level of aspiration and behavior in manic-depressive psychoses. *Univ. Ia. Stud. Child-Welf.*, 1940, *16*, No. 3, 199–302.

FARSON, R. E. Praise reappraised. *Harvard Bus. Rev.*, 1963, *41*, 61–66.

FESTINGER, L. A theory of social comparison processes. *Hum. Relat.*, 1954, *7*, 117–140.

FESTINGER, L. *A theory of cognitive dissonance.* Evanston: Row, 1957.

FESTINGER, L. & FREEDMAN, J. Dissonance reduction and moral values. In P. Worchel and D. Byrne (Eds.), *Personality change.* New York: Wiley, 1964.

FREUD, S. *Group psychology and the analysis of the ego.* London: Hogarth, 1922. (Translated from *Massenpsychologie und Ich-Analyse*, Vienna, 1921.)

GERARD, H. B. Inconsistency of beliefs and their implications. Paper read at American Psychological Assn., New York, September 1961. (a)

GERARD, H. B. Some determinants of self-evaluation. *J. abnorm. soc. Psychol.*, 1961, *62*, 288–293. (b)

GERARD, H. B. & GREENBAUM, C. W. Attitudes toward an agent of uncertainty reduction. *J. Pers.*, 1962, *30*, 485–495.

GERGEN, K. J. Interaction goals and personalistic feedback as factors affecting the presentation of the self. Unpublished doctoral dissertation, Duke University, 1962.

GEWIRTZ, J. L. & BAER, D. M. Deprivation and satiation of social reinforcers as drive conditions. *J. abnorm. soc. Psychol.*, 1958, *57*, 165–172.

GOFFMAN, E. On face-work. *Psychiatry*, 1955, *18*, 213–231.

GOFFMAN, E. *The presentation of self in everyday life.* New York: Doubleday, 1959.

HEIDER, F. Attitudes and cognitive organization. *J. Psychol.*, 1946, *21*, 107–112.

HEIDER, F. *The psychology of interpersonal relations.* New York: Wiley, 1958.

HOMANS, G. C. *Social behavior: its elementary forms.* New York: Harcourt, 1961.

JOHNSON, S. *Lives of the poets.* (vol. I) New York: Doubleday, n.d. (originally published in 1779).

JONES, E. E., GERGEN, K. J. & DAVIS, K. E. Some determinants of reactions to being approved or disapproved as a person. *Psychol. Monogr.*, 1962, 76, Whole No. 521.

JONES, E. E., GERGEN, K. J., GUMPERT, P. & THIBAUT, J. W. Some conditions affecting the use of ingratiation to influence performance evaluation. *J. abnorm. soc. Psychol.*, in press.

JONES, E. E., GERGEN, K. J. & JONES, R. G. Tactics of ingratiation among leaders and subordinates in a status hierarchy. *Psychol. Monogr.*, 1963, 77, Whole No. 566.

JONES, E. E., HESTER, S. L., FARINA, A. & DAVIS, K. E. Reactions to unfavorable personal evaluations as a function of the evaluator's perceived adjustment. *J. abnorm. soc. Psychol.*, 1959, 59, 363–370.

JONES, E. E., JONES, R. G. & GERGEN, K. J. Some conditions affecting the evaluation of a conformist. *J. Pers.*, 1963, 31, 270–288.

JONES, R. G. & JONES, E. E. Optimum conformity as an ingratiation tactic. *J. Pers.*, 1964, 32, 436–458.

MILLS, J. Changes in moral attitudes following temptation, *J. Pers.*, 1958, 26, 517–531.

NEWCOMB, T. M. The prediction of interpersonal attraction. *Amer. Psychologist*, 1956, 11, 575–586.

NEWCOMB, T. M. *The acquaintance process.* New York: Holt, 1961.

PLUTARCH. *Plutarch's miscellanies and essays.* (W. W. Goodwin, Ed.) vol. II. Boston: Little, Brown, 1889. (Originally written c. 100.)

RIESMAN, D. *The lonely crowd.* New Haven: Yale, 1958.

ROSENBAUM, M. E. & DeCHARMS, R. Direct and vicarious reduction of hostility. *J. abnorm. soc. Psychol.*, 1960, 60, 105–112.

ROTTER, J. B. *Social learning and clinical psychology.* New York: Prentice-Hall, 1954.

SCHACHTER, S. Deviation, rejection, and communication. *J. abnorm. soc. Psychol.*, 1951, 46, 190–207.

STEVENSON, B. *The home book of quotations.* New York: Dodd, 1934.

SWANSON, G. E., NEWCOMB, T. M. & HARTLEY, E. L. (Eds.) *Readings in social psychology* (rev.) New York: Holt, 1952.

TAGIURI, R. & PETRULLO, L. *Person perception and interpersonal behavior.* Stanford: Stanford Univ., 1958.

THIBAUT, J. W. & KELLEY, H. H. *The social psychology of groups.* New York: Wiley, 1959.

THIBAUT, J. W. & RIECKEN, H. W. Some determinants and consequences of the perception of social causality. *J. Pers.*, 1955, *24*, 113–133.

TOLMAN, E. C. Principles of performance. *Psychol. Rev.*, 1955, *62*, 315–326.

WEBB, E. T. & MORGAN, J. B. *Strategy in handling people*. Garden City, L.I.: Garden City Publ., 1930.

Author Index

Subject Index